DEBRETT'S

MANNERS AND CORRECT FORM IN THE MIDDLE EAST

SIR DONALD HAWLEY, KCMG, MBE

DEBRETT'S PEERAGE LIMITED
LONDON · NEW YORK · TORONTO · SYDNEY
in association with
THE BRITISH BANK OF THE MIDDLE EAST

© Sir Donald Hawley, 1984

First published in 1984

Published by Debrett's Peerage Limited,
73-77 Britannia Road, London SW6 2JR
in association with
The British Bank of the Middle East,
a member of the Hongkong Bank Group

Distributed by J.M. Dent & Sons (Distribution) Ltd,
Dunhams Lane, Letchworth, Herts, SG6 1LF

Typeset by Midas Publishing Services, Oxford
Printed in Great Britain at the Pitman Press, Bath

ISBN 0 905649 67 2

Contents

Foreword

by Sir Geoffrey Arthur

In the first paragraph of his guide to manners in the Arab world Sir Donald Hawley has written all the introduction that is necessary: the ill-mannered man is not forgiven, and, however well-intentioned he may be, he will fail.

I look back with secret shame on the occasions when I have been unmindful of my own advice. I have lost good causes and sometimes good friends too. Most of these unhappy episodes have been the sour fruits of impatience, for it is easy to forget, in this age when the Arabs have taken to jet aircraft as readily as the rest of us, that the tempo of life in the Middle East is in some important ways different from the one to which we have become accustomed in Europe and America. The visitor who expects to conduct his business briskly and immediately is likely to be disappointed: patience, which is one of the foundations of good manners anywhere in the world, is of particular importance in Arabia. That the Arabs are not often in a hurry is one of the reasons why their own manners are so good.

All this is common knowledge, though it often goes unregarded. We can also give offence unintentionally, through ignorance of foreign customs and beliefs. The guest in a strange house needs to know what to expect. When I told a friend that another of my friends had written a short guide to Arab customs, his response was immediate – "Ah! You mean sheep's eyes and all that." As Sir Donald Hawley implies, the persistence of the sheep's eye story is probably only to be explained by the practical jokes which Englishmen, with Arab connivance, play on each other. It is not entirely a myth: forty years ago in southern Iraq I have seen sheep's eyes eaten, indeed have tried one myself; but even then very few tribes ate the head of the sheep, and only two I knew offered it to their guests. I have never seen an eye, on my or anybody else's plate, since 1945.

So the reader may forget the sheep's eye: unless he is concerned for his weight he will enjoy Arab food. But there is plenty of what the friend I have quoted called "all that" – the small courtesies or offences which may be unknown in the West. In the past most of us had to learn these things the hard way. I shall never forget being reproved in public for showing the soles of my shoes to the governor of a province of Iraq. Now that one rarely has to sit cross-legged on the floor, one is less likely to commit this particular solecism. But there are many other such matters on which visitors, and especially those whose stay must be short, need help. Sir Donald Hawley's book gives such guidance as is possible (for local variations are great, and times are changing) on protocol, on forms of address, both oral and written, as well as on Arab manners, customs and beliefs. I wish it had been available when I was new to the Middle East. I recommend it strongly to all western residents or visitors.

Preface

It may be useful to start with some explanation of what this book is not. It is not a comprehensive work on the social and other customs of the Middle East. This would require an encyclopaedia. It is not an infallible guide to behaviour, because the area is so vast and diverse in character and the situations which a traveller to the Middle East may meet are so numerous and varied that they are incapable of reduction to copybook answers. The book is not intended for those who know Arabic and the ways of Arabia and it is not a learned disquisition on Islam, its philosophy and practice. It is not for scholars.

It is, however, designed to give some general guidance on customs, behaviour and attitudes in the modern Middle East, and some terms in Arabic or concerning Islam, which are liable to come up or be heard, are introduced. It is thus a book with modest pretentions but it is written in the hope that it may be helpful in avoiding the worst pitfalls.

I am most grateful to those who have kindly helped by reading the manuscript or parts of it and offered their comments, in particular Sir Geoffrey Arthur, who has also kindly written the Foreword, Sir Philip Adams, Sir Richard Beaumont, Sir James Craig, Mr St John Armitage, Mr Raymond Flower, and Mr Easa Gurg. I am also most grateful to a number of kind friends in H.M. Diplomatic Service. However, the responsibility for any error is mine and mine alone.

Donald Hawley

NOTE ON TRANSLITERATION

Although opinions vary widely on how Arabic names and words should be put into English, a choice is necessary unless one adopts the whimsical, free for all approach of T.E. Lawrence. I have, therefore, tried to make the transliteration as close as possible to the sound one expects from a normal reading of the English. Broadly, vowels in Arabic words used in this book are pronounced as follows:–

a   as in Pa
i   as in seen
u   as in soon
o   as in own
ai as in hay

However, I have not included any sign to show that a vowel should be lengthened, as such signs tend to be slightly disruptive to the text.

In transliterating one of the holy places of Islam, I have adopted the spelling Makkah, the official version in Saudi Arabia, rather than Mecca. In all other cases of words terminating in a (or ah), I have omitted the final h.

Chapter 1

The Middle East and the Arab World

William of Wykeham, the founder of Winchester and New College Oxford, gave them both his motto 'Manners Makyth Man'. This precept, in the sense in which it was intended, is now less regarded in Britain and the West than formerly. However, lack of knowledge of local manners may not only mar a trip to the Middle East but also wreck chances of doing business and damage the reputation of an individual and his country. To call a man mannerless is regarded as a very great insult in the Arab world, though the Malays carry the thought even further with their proverb that:

'It is better even that a child should die
than that manners should be forfeited.'

However, the first thing is to be clear on the terms 'Middle East' and 'Arab World'. The term 'Middle East', originally a British invention based on political and military definitions of areas of influence, is now a generally accepted term in the East and elsewhere. Logically it might seem to signify the area between the Near and Far East and might have been thought to apply to the Indian sub-continent. However, the usage began in the heyday of British imperial power when the Indian Empire with its British administration and British-officered Indian Army was regarded as a projection of Britain itself. The term 'Middle East' was, therefore, applied to part of the area between Europe and India. The Royal Institute of International Affairs, Chatham House, puts it as follows:

> Before the First World War it was customary to distinguish between the Near East comprising Greece, Bulgaria, Turkey, The Levant and Egypt; and the Middle East, Arabia, Mesopotamia (now Iraq), the Gulf, Persia and Afghanistan. It then gradually became the practice to use the term 'Middle East' to cover both those areas, less Greece and Bulgaria on the West and Afghanistan on the east, but adding the Sudan and sometimes Libya and even other North African states.

Professor W.B. Fisher, a leading Geographer of the Middle East, says that the term denotes the territories of 'Egypt and the Sudan, Turkey, Iran, Libya, and Arabian peninsula and intermediate regions'. The term is, therefore, not precisely synonymous with the 'Arab World' because it includes such non-Arab countries as Iran and Turkey. However, by the term 'Middle East' I am alluding particularly to the Arab countries – 'The Arab World' – though much of what is said also has some relevance in Iran and Turkey and among the Arabs in Israel.

It is sometimes said that the Arabian fable of the frog and the scorpion illustrates the unpredictable and paradoxical nature of Middle Eastern politics:

> A scorpion on the banks of the Nile asked a frog to ferry him to the other side. The frog, not trusting the scorpion, replied "No, you'll sting

me". "Nonsense," said the scorpion. "Why should I sting you when I cannot swim myself and we would both be drowned?" Confronted with this logic, the frog reluctantly agreed and set off across the river with the scorpion on his back. In mid-stream the scorpion stung the frog, who angrily asked why he had done it. As they both floundered the scorpion, with his last breath, said "Ah, frog, you forget. This is the Middle East!"

However, no such doubt or paradox exists about the customs and manners of the region, which are both understandable and predictable.

Islam, like other monotheistic religions, which it respects, came out of Arabia. But Islam regards the Koran as the final Revelation and Muhammad as the Prophet to whom Allah, the one true God, made this divine revelation. Islam, therefore, colours the thoughts and behaviour of nearly everyone there and phrases with religious meaning, or overtones, are in day to day use. Nonetheless some degree of ambivalence between what is required by religion and custom on the one hand and actual private behaviour on the other is a common a feature in the Middle East as in other parts of the world.

Even in the society of sophisticated and westernised people in the Middle East, gratuitous personal comments on Islam, or religion generally, or on local habits and customs should be avoided, at least until the stage in acquaintance is reached when frank philosophical or religious discussion is both possible and safe. Respect for and knowledge of other people's customs and traditions may be rewarding as well as courteous.

Varying customs in respect of women prevail in different countries and at different levels in each society. The traditional place of women is in the home and throughout the Arab World their principal role remains there with no moving in mixed society. Further there is a special part of the home set aside for them – the harim (also see Chapter 8). Their main roles are providing food for husband and male visitors, bringing up the small children of both sexes and looking after the older unmarried girls. Their society outside the home lies with other women. Women always have a segregated part of a mosque and in many countries there is strict segregation of the sexes at public functions.

However, at the other end of the scale educated women in such countries as Egypt and Iraq play a prominent part in public life, unthinkable in other countries, and some of them hold ministerial and high official office. In most of the major cities there are considerable numbers of people, men and women, who see no inconsistency between mixed social, as well as official, contact and Islam. But the very liberal attitudes of the West are not generally admired and western measures against sex discrimination would not be in tune with either male or female attitudes in the area.

The use of female bodyguards in Libya is unusual and goes far beyond what custom would accept in most Arab countries.

The ethos of the particular country one may be in towards women is, therefore, important and it is equally important to know, or find out, the attitude towards segregation which an Arab friend might hold in connection with his wife and female members of the family.

The language of the Koran is Arabic and Islam is essentially the religion of the Arab world, though it has also been embraced in many other countries — Indonesia, Malaysia, Pakistan, Bangladesh, India, Iran, and some African countries. A revival of fundamental Islamic ideas and ideals, affecting people's attitudes, dress and day to day behaviour, has recently occurred in many of these countries — a revival which is at least in part a reaction to permissive standards introduced from the West.

Though the Arab world comprises many countries, the people share a common inheritance both in the Koran and the Arab language generally, despite local variations and dialects. They are also all very aware of a common culture and Arab Nationalism, concepts of Arabism and a sense of affinity affect them all in some measure. Consciousness that the growth of Israel is central to Middle Eastern politics and has resulted in injustice to the Palestinians, fellow Arabs, is general and, though there are many views about the rights and wrongs of this, Jerusalem is as important to Muslims as to Christians and Jews; they believe that it was from there that the Prophet Muhammad made his ascent into Heaven.

In parts of Arabia the day is still occasionally calculated in Arabic time, and the hours of the day start from sunset. Thus one hour after sunset, at whatever time this may be, is one o'clock of the new day — several hours before midnight Western time. This is important especially in relation to Muslim feasts and fasts, which are moveable in the sense that they are calculated by the moon.

It is wise to ascertain when certain Muslim feasts and the month-long Fast of Ramadan fall, for no business is done over the feasts any more than it is over Christmas in the West, and, though work continues, local patterns of life change during Ramadan when strict Muslims do not eat and drink between sunrise and sunset.

Western ways and habits, though adopted to a greater or lesser extent by many, particularly the western-educated people, in all Middle East countries, are not universally admired and, if due consideration is not shown, may cause offence. Generally, people are in some ways more strait-laced and puritanical in public behaviour than in the West. Dirty jeans, shaggy hair and decaying gym shoes are not admired; nor are shorts. Sophisticated Arabs, men and women, nowadays often tend to be smarter, more discriminating in taste and better groomed than many modern Anglo-Saxons.

Arabs are very conscious, in an age of technology, that their civilization, while Europe was in the Dark Ages following the collapse of the Roman Empire, kept alive the torch of learning. They not only transmitted the science, mathematics and philosophy of the Greeks and Romans to the Renaissance and modern generations in the West, but also produced many notable innovations and inventions – the astrolabe is an example – of their own. Many words in everyday use too come from the Arabic, for example admiral, alchemy, algebra, sugar and lemon, to name a few.

Observation of correct form in the Middle East is helped by bearing all this in mind and, in particular, some understanding of Islam is required.

Chapter 2

Islam —
Belief, Festivals and Fasts

General

Islam is, as we have seen, the predominant religion of
the Middle East and is essentially the religion of the
Arabs, though most of its 500 or more million adherents in fact live outside the Arab world and there
are Arabs who are not Muslims.

Many states in the Middle East have secular constitu-
tions, but Islam does not distinguish fundamentally
between sacred and secular matters; Islam's philosophy is, in effect, part of the theology. Conceptually
religion and law are one and the same and religious
and secular authority are also one, well illustrated by
the fact that the green national flag of Saudi Arabia
bears the words 'There is no God but God (Allah) and
Muhammad is his prophet'. However, despite this
most Middle Eastern countries do have bodies of legislation, for example concerning crime and commercial
matters, which are secular in form and application and
in many of the countries there are established civil
courts and civil codes separate from the Islamic –
Sharia – jurisdiction.

The practice of Islam – the word means submission
to God – is based on the Koran (alternative spellings
are: Quran and Kuran). The original and authentic

text of this book of divine revelation forms the basis of all Islamic education in the Arabic language and is read throughout the Muslim world in mosques, in schools, on the radio and on television even where Arabic is not spoken. The basic tenet is the oneness of God and the belief that the Prophet Muhammad was divinely inspired.

Pillars of Islam

There are five 'pillars' of Islam imposing five duties on every Muslim:

1. *IMAN* (or *SHIHADA*), profession of faith: this involves saying with full acceptance 'There is no god but God and Muhammad is his prophet'.

2. *SALAT*, Prayer: this involves praying five times daily, facing Makkah (Mecca) and saying Friday noonday prayers in the mosque.

3. *ZAKAT*, alms tax: this involves payment of the charitable tax payable by Muslims. But the giving of alms beyond this is also regarded as meritorious.

4. *RAMADAN:* this involves keeping the fast, Sōm, in the holy month of Ramadan.

5. *HAJJ*, pilgrimage: this means, if possible, at least once making the pilgrimage, the Hajj, to Makkah and the other holy places of Islam.

Prayers

The five compulsory prayers are:–

> *Salat as-Subh* or *Salat al Fajr* – morning or dawn
> prayer
> *Salat ad Dhuhr* – midday prayer
> *Salat al Asr* – afternoon prayer
> *Salat al Mughrib* – sunset prayer
> *Salat al Isha* – evening prayer (about two hours
> after sunset)

From the minarets of mosques all over the Islamic
world muezzins call the people to prayer, nowadays
often through loudspeakers, at these times.

Prayers do not, however, need to be said in a
mosque, though they often are, but may be recited
in a dwelling house or elsewhere. It is not uncommon
for a Muslim to excuse himself at the appropriate time,
even during a meeting, to go to another room or to
another part of the same room to say prayers. These
are nearly always said on a special prayer mat which is
rolled out to face Makkah. Ritual ablution and certain
postures as well as specific verses of the Koran are pre-
scribed for these prayers. Friday, the Muslim holiday,
is the day when there are special prayers at the mosque
in the morning and it is known as '*Yom al juma*' – the
day of congregation. Prayers are led by the Imam.

Islamic Teaching

Muslim teaching is based not only on the Koran but
also on the Sunna of the Prophet as recorded in the

Hadith (Traditions of the Prophet's sayings and do-
ings handed down by his companions, exemplifying
the practice of Islam). There are four orthodox
schools of Muslim jurisprudence – the Hanafi, Han-
bali, Maliki and Shafi, named after their founders Abu
Hanifa, Ahmad ibn Hanbal, Malik ibn Anas and
Muhammad Idris al Shafi.

Islamic (Sharia) Law

In some Muslim countries all law administered is
Islamic – the Sharia law is based both on the Koran itself and the Hadith – and the only courts are Sharia, or
Islamic courts, even though modern legislation and
custom may have been grafted on to traditional law. In
others, however, the Islamic law applies to all personal
cases affecting Muslims and the secular civil, criminal
or commercial law is applied to all inhabitants. In such
countries special provision is made for the private
personal law of non-Muslims.

Sunni and Shia

The two great sections of the Muslim community are
the Sunni and the Shia and there are differences of
emphasis between them. The division originally came
over the succession to the Prophet Muhammad, who
lived from about 570 to 632 A.D. On the Prophet's
death Abu Bakr, a merchant of Makkah, was chosen as
the Caliph or successor and he held office from 632 to

634, being succeeded by Omar (634 to 644) and Othman (644 to 656). However, some people who later formed themselves into the Shia sect considered that Ali – a cousin of Muhammad, who had been brought up by him as a son and who had married the Prophet's daughter Fatima – was the true Caliph and that only those from his line were legitimate successors to the Caliphate. In fact Ali became Caliph in 656 in succession to Othman but was defeated at the battle of Siffin on the Euphrates by Muawiya, who assumed the Caliphate. Later, in 680, Ali's son Hussain was killed near Kerbala in the 'Battle of the Camel' on the 10th Muharram, a day which the Shia still commemorate as a day of mourning and repentance.

The Muslim Calendar

The Muslim calendar is a religious one and, like earlier Arabian calendars, is based on the movements of the moon. The Prophet Muhammad said 'A year is 12 months as at the time of the creation.' Thus the year consists of 12 lunar months and the practice followed under the old Arabian calendar, whereby an additional 13th month was added every third year in order to try and keep the lunar and the solar years related, was abandoned and is no longer followed.

In relation to the solar year, the Muslim calendar moves back approximately 11 days every year and thus every 32½ years it recovers its relative position. However, the 11 day difference is neither precise nor entirely regular and, according to the actual time of the moon's changes in the solar year, it sometimes has to be reckoned as 10 days and sometimes 12.

In most Arab countries the new month does not, as we have seen, begin until the new moon has been sighted in that particular territory. This sighting is of special significance at the beginning of the fasting month of *Ramadan* and the next month, *Shawwal*, when the Id al Fitr, the festival of the breaking of the fast, is celebrated. It is never possible to tell in advance on which precise day the new moon, *Hilal,* will be sighted in a given territory.

The Muslim months are:–

> *Muharram*
> *Safar*
> *Rabi al awal*
> *Rabi al akhir* (or *al thani*)
> *Jamada al ula*
> *Jamada al ukhra*
> *Rajab*
> *Shaban*
> *Ramadan*
> *Shawwal*
> *Dhu al qada*
> *Dhu al Hijja*

The days of the week are:–

Yom al ahad	Sunday
Yom al ithnain	Monday
Yom al thalata	Tuesday
Yom al arbaa	Wednesday
Yom al khamis	Thursday
Yom al jumaa	Friday
Yom al sabit	Saturday

The Muslim Era

Years in the Muslim world are reckoned from the 'Hijra', when the Prophet Muhammad emigrated to Medina in 622 A.D. It was from this time that his influence and strength began to wax. Consequently the lunar years since that date are referred to as A.H., i.e. after the 'Hijra'. Since they are lunar years they do not correspond exactly with the solar years of the Gregorian calendar and reference to books which give the nearly corresponding years is necessary. 1400 A.H. fell, for example, in the Gregorian year 1980.

In the earlier days of Islam, Muslims named the years by descriptions, e.g. 'The year of the earthquake' and 'the year of farewell' but in about 17 A.H. (in 639 A.D.) the Caliph Omar decided that the Muslim era should date from the first day of the first month, *Muharram*, of the year in which the 'Hijra' took place.

The Feasts and Celebrations of Islam*

ISLAMIC (HIJRA) NEW YEAR

The Muslim New Year is celebrated on the first of *Muharram*, which was fixed at the first month of the year in the Koran.

PROPHET MUHAMMAD'S BIRTHDAY (MULID AN NABI)

This is the celebration of the birthday of the Prophet Muhammad, who was born in Makkah on a date not

---

* Not all are celebrated in all Arab or Islamic countries.

precisely known though 570 AD and 580 AD are both considered possible.

The Prophet's birthday is traditionally celebrated on the 12th of *Rabi al awal*. In some parts of the Muslim world it is a great festival, featuring torchlight processions, feasting and fairs in the streets with the chanting of *zikrs* (dhikrs) in honour of Allah and the Prophet and the recitation of *Mulids*, panegyrical poems on the birth and life of the Prophet, extolling his virtues.

THE NIGHT JOURNEY AND ASCENSION

Lailat al isra wa al miraj is observed on the 27th of *Rajab*. It commemorates the Prophet Muhammad's night journey and ascent into heaven. This is referred to in the Koran, and the main tradition is that it took place from Jerusalem. During the Prophet's ascension, which reputedly took place in his lifetime and occurred shortly after his call as a Prophet, he is believed to have met Allah face to face in the Seventh Heaven, and to have received instruction about the obligatory prayers of Islam. These include the public prayers at the *Id* festivals (see below) and the five daily prayers.

RAMADAN

Ramadan is observed all over the Muslim world as the month of fasting. This involves taking no food or drink or, amongst the strictest, even swallowing during the hours between sunrise and sunset. During this month Muslims usually take a light meal accompanied by soft drinks shortly after sunset and a heavier meal a little later. Another meal is also eaten in the small hours of the morning well before sunrise.

Ramadan is generally declared on the authority of the chief Muslim lawmaker, usually the Mufti, that the time is due. Normally two witnesses of truth have to satisfy the Chief *Kadi* (Judge) that they have seen the new moon with their own eyes. In some cases nowadays, however, a State will follow its neighbours, dispensing with the earlier requirement that the new moon must have been sighted in the actual territory where the fast is declared. It still often happens, however, that *Ramadan* is declared on different days in different, even neighbouring, states. The same procedure is followed for the sighting of the new moon after *Ramadan* and the declaration of the feast of *Id al Fitr*.

During the fasting month of *Ramadan* people may be less accessible, owing to the different pattern of life during this month, and sometimes there is a general slowing down of the pace of life. This is particularly so when *Ramadan* falls during the hot summer months and fasting imposes a greater strain than when it falls in the shorter days of winter.

IDS

Id denotes one of the two 'canonical' Muslim festivals, *Id al Adha* and *Id al Fitr*. At both *Ids* calls are made and frequently too presents are given. The word is derived by Arab lexicographers from the Arabic word meaning 'to return' and connotes a periodically returning event. The two *Ids* are:–

Id al Fitr

Id al Fitr, also known in the Arab world as *Id as Saghir*, or *Ramadan Bairam*, is proclaimed when the new moon is seen at the end of the month of *Ramadan*, during which fasting between sunrise and sunset is enjoined for Muslims. The name of the feast denotes the breaking of the fast and, although it is strictly the lesser of the two *Id* festivals, it is often celebrated more wholeheartedly as a result of the strain of fasting being relieved.

Id al Adha

Id al Adha, meaning the feast of the sacrifice, is celebrated on the 10th of *Dhu al Hijja* – 39 or 40 days after the first day of *Id al Fitr*. The pilgrimage (*Hajj*) ceremonies reach their climax on this and the two succeeding days at Mina near Makkah when every pilgrim sacrifices a sheep (or camel or cattle) commemorating Abraham's willingness to sacrifice his son's life to God and the providential appearance of the sheep. The animal slaughtered must be of a certain age and free from physical defects. Muslims all over the world are bound to sacrifice at this time. The period of sacrifice starts after the *Id* prayers (*Salat al Id*, festival of public prayer for the whole community) and ends at sunset on the 3rd of the 3 days. The sacrificial ceremony should include blessing on the Prophet, turning towards the *kibla* (the direction of Makkah) and a request for acceptance of the sacrifice.

10TH MUHARRAM (ASHURA)

This is observed as a day of mourning by the Shia. It is the anniversary of the battle of Kerbala in 680 AD at which Hussain bin Ali bin Abu Talib, who was the sole surviving grandson of the Prophet, was killed fighting against the Omayyad Caliph, Yazid bin Muawiya. Hussain's father, Ali, was the Prophet's cousin and son-in-law, having married his daughter Fatima. The Shia believe that the rightful succession to the Caliphate lay with Ali and subsequently his sons Hassan and Hussain rather than with Muawiya and his son Yazid. Consequently, 10th *Muharram* is observed as a day of mourning and marked by pilgrimages to the Shia holy places, especially Kerbala, where a passion play is enacted representing the death of Ali's sons, Hussain and Hassan, who had predeceased his brother.

Ashura is also observed as an optional fast, theologically classified as 'commendable' by the Sunnis, for entirely different reasons. The fast is based on ancient traditions about the significance of the day – such as that on this day Noah left the ark and Adam met Eve after they had been cast out of the Garden of Eden.

SAUDI ARABIA

In Saudi Arabia only *Id al Fitr* and *Id al Adha* are celebrated as holidays.

NATIONAL DAYS

The National Days celebrated in each country are not usually related to religious festivals.

The Pilgrimage

The *Hajj*, or the pilgrimage, being one of the five pillars of Islam, has a special place in Muslim thinking and actions. All Muslims aspire to make the pilgrimage once in their lifetime to Makkah and the holy places now in Saudi Arabia and many millions achieve it, thus acquiring the right and privilege of being called *Hajji*. In 1982 for instance it was calculated that there were 2.2 millions pilgrims. These holy places may only be visited by Muslims.

For centuries there were yearly pilgrim caravans from Egypt, Syria, Persia, Iraq and the Maghreb to the holy places, the pilgrims mounted on camels, horses and donkeys or on foot. By tradition a splendid covering, called the *Kiswa*, was woven every year in Egypt and embroidered with texts from the Koran and brought to the great Mosque at Makkah to cover the Kaaba, the building in the centre of the courtyard which is the oldest site of monotheism for collective prayers known on earth. The *Kiswa* is now provided by Saudi Arabia.

Today most pilgrims travel by air and, although the pilgrimage is a highly organised religious occasion, it remains a physically taxing experience even for the able-bodied. The pilgrims are accompanied on the sacred rites (*manasik*) of the pilgrimage by special traditional guides, called *Mutawwafin*.

The *Hajj* has been described as 'an annual reminder of the continuity of the message of the ONE GOD through successive Prophets' and it is made to a place very closely associated with the Prophet Ibrahim, better known as Abraham in the West.

The Koran describes the sacred *Kaaba* as the first temple ever set up for mankind, 'rich in blessing and a source of guidance to all the worlds .... a place where Ibrahim once stood ... whoever enters it finds peace.' Many of the rites of the pilgrimage are based on traditions concerning Ibrahim and his son Ismail (Ishmael).

In order to denote their state as well as to create a spirit of unity and equality, all pilgrims are dressed in the *ihram* dress. The state of *ihram* implies a prohibition of certain actions during the pilgrimage and the dress consists of two new, plain white, unsewn garments, one covering the lower part of the body and the other the upper. The putting on of these clothes marks the beginning of the *Hajj*, after which prayers are said. After this comes the first of the seven *Tawaf* (circling of the *Kaaba*), followed by prayers at Maqam Ibrahim, 'the place of Ibrahim', a small structure also within the precincts of the Great Mosque. It contains a sacred stone on which Ibrahim is said to have stood when laying the foundation of the *Kaaba* itself and which is believed to have preserved the imprint of the patriarch's foot. Near this many of the companions of the Prophet Muhammad are buried.

The sacred well of Zamzam is also in the courtyard and water from it is ceremonially drunk as part of the *Hajj*, commemorating its discovery by Hagar and her son Ismail, which prevented them from dying of thirst in the desert.

On the eighth day of *Dhu al Hijja*, the month of the pilgrimage, the pilgrims go to Mina and on the following day to Arafat – both are close to Makkah – for the *Wakfa*, a universal meeting of all the pilgrims on a high arid plain. They then leave for Muzdafila, between

Mina and Mount Ararat, where they arrive for the sunset prayer. They return to Mina on the following day for the ceremonial stoning of the devil, Satan, represented by three pillars of stone. After casting seven stones at the pillars, all the pilgrims sacrifice their own sacrificial animals. This ceremony concludes the pilgrimage. Pilgrims then shave, the *ihram* dress is removed and they may bathe. Before leaving Makkah the pilgrim makes a final circuit of the *Kaaba* and may drink of the water of the Zamzam well at this stage.

The visits to the mosque and grave of the Prophet Muhammad at Medina are not a part of the pilgrimage but most pilgrims regard them as an incumbent duty.

Chapter 3

Modes of Address

General

Both oral and written forms of address in the Middle East are more formal and flowery than in Anglo-Saxon countries nowadays. Virtually all forms of spoken address in Arabic are preceded by *'Ya'*, the Arabic equivalent of 'O'. Examples from various countries are *'Ya akhi'* – 'O, my brother/friend'; *'Ya aini'* – 'O, my eye', i.e. dear one or dear friend*: or at a more exalted level *'Ya hadrat sahib al Saada'* – 'O, Your Presence, Lord of Felicity'.

In many countries, especially Egypt, Sudan and the central part of the Middle East one never addresses anyone, however lowly in the local social scale, otherwise than with an honorific, e.g. *'Ya Rais'* – 'O, Chief' to a man who has looked after your car in a car park; or *'Ya Osta'*† – 'O, Expert' to someone who has cleaned the windows. On the other hand in parts of Arabia where Bedu traditions remain strong, forms of address may be more direct *'Ya, Ahmad'* – 'O, Ahmad', though the usage of the great cities of the Middle East such as Cairo, Baghdad, Beirut and Damascus has now spread further afield. Even though titles were abolished after

---

* Widely and commonly used to both sexes in Iraq.

† More correctly *Ustadh* (or *Ustaz*): teacher (see p. 50) but used in the form *'Osta'* in Egypt and the Sudan.

the fall of King Farouk and the abolition of the Egyptian monarchy, '*Ya, Bey*' – 'O, Bey' is still very frequently used amongst the Egyptians and even '*Ya, Pasha*' – 'O, Pasha' to someone clearly higher in rank.

This, however, merely demonstrates the flavour of speech and does not solve the dilemma of the English speaker. More specific advice, therefore, follows.

Language

In considering how to address any important personage in the Middle East, it is advisable to take local advice on whether the particular communication is best made in Arabic or whether it can be made in English or French. If Arabic is to be used, a competent translator should be engaged locally. Arabs from one country who are working in another may not always be infallible advisers on the niceties of local custom and usage.

Where communication is not in Arabic, French styles of address generally apply in countries formerly under French influence, while English forms are used in the countries formerly within the British sphere of influence. In Libya, formerly under Italian control, there are special considerations.

Kings and the Sultan of Oman

The King of Saudi Arabia, the King of Jordan, the King of Morocco and the Sultan of Oman are to a greater or lesser extent involved in the government of their countries and are, therefore, distinguishable

onstitutional monarchs elsewhere. This has
earing on forms of address because direct com-
tion in the course of business will not in-
tly arise. The names of the various dynasties
en in Appendix B.

usual manner of addressing a King or the Sul-
through the court official responsible and, if a
unication comes from such an official, the reply
d be to him. It is best to enquire locally about the
ct title of the particular official. However, most
spondence is addressed to or emanates from the
l Protocol Office. Details of the respective officers
given in Appendix C.

here may be exceptional cases where it is approp-
e to write direct to the King or Sultan. For example
s may be done by people whose personal friendship
general relationship with the monarch is such as to
spire confidence that the direct address would not be
nwelcome. In such cases the following direct forms of
address may be used:

OPENING OF LETTER

'Your Majesty', after which any of the following may be
used:

'After greetings (or compliments)'
'May I respectfully present my greetings/compliments
and ..... (inform, advise, etc) Your Majesty that.....'

BODY OF LETTER

In the body of the letter 'Your Majesty' should generally be used for 'you' and 'Your Majesty's' for 'yours'.

ENDING OF LETTERS

The following forms, which conform to usage
Arabic, are possible:

'Please accept, Your Majesty, the assurances of m
highest respect (and consideration)'
or
'Finally, Your Majesty, may I offer my profound re
spects'.

A more personal ending may be substituted by some
one who enjoys the monarch's personal friendship
The signature must be clear and legible.

ENVELOPE

The envelope should be addressed:—

'His Majesty King (Sultan).....'

ORAL ADDRESS

The Sovereign should normally be addressed as 'Your
Majesty' in the first instance, though it is permissible,
thereafter, generally to address him as 'Sir'. Similarly if
one is referring to a Sovereign, he should be referred
to in conversation as 'His Majesty'. In Arabic this is
'*Jalalat al Malik*' for a King and '*Jalalat as Sultan*' for the
Sultan of Oman*

---

* It was a long and endearing custom that until 1971 the Sultan
of Muscat and Oman used to be addressed by the British Representative as 'Dear Friend' and he likewise used to address the
British Representative similarly. This fell into disuse when
Oman became more directly involved in world affairs and
joined the United Nations and the Arab League. This pleasant
custom was also followed in the Sultanate of Brunei.

Amirs and Rulers in the Gulf

In the Gulf area the Amirs (Rulers) of Kuwait, Bahrain and Qatar are, like the Kings and the Sultan, sovereign Heads of State. The United Arab Emirates is a federation of seven states each ruled by a different Ruler and the Head of the Federal State is a President elected by the Rulers from amongst themselves, at present the Ruler of Abu Dhabi.

The general rules about addressing Amirs are the same as those suggested above in relation to Kings and the Sultan of Oman, except that in general the ceremony and protocol surrounding Gulf Rulers is of an Arab traditional nature, Bedu in origin, and not markedly rigid. All the Amirs and Rulers are addressed in Arabic, as is the King of Saudi Arabia, by saying 'May God prolong your life' – *'Tawal amrak'* or *'Ya tawil al amr'**.

The following forms of address are appropriate:–

OPENING OF LETTER

'Your Highness' after which the following may be used:

'May I respectfully present my greetings and ..... (inform, advise, etc) Your Highness that .....'
'After greetings .....'

BODY OF THE LETTER

In the body of the letter 'Your Highness' should generally be used instead of 'you' and 'Your Highness's' for 'yours'.

---

* cf. 'Oh, King! Live for ever'.

ENDING OF LETTER

The following forms or near equivalents are possible:
'Please accept, Your Highness, the assurances of my highest respect (and consideration)'
or
'Finally, Your Highness, may I offer my profound respects'
or
'Finally, Your Highness, I take this opportunity to renew assurances of my highest consideration'.

ENVELOPE

The envelope should be addressed:

'His Highness Shaikh ..... bin .....
Amir (or in the United Arab Emirates, Ruler) of .....'

or (in case of the President of the United Arab Emirates)
'His Highness President Shaikh .....
The Presidential Palace
.....'

When Rulers of the individual states of the United Arab Emirates are addressed, they are addressed in the same manner as the other Rulers in the Gulf, the Amirs, other than the President of the United Arab Emirates (U.A.E.).

ORAL ADDRESS

All Rulers and the President of the United Arab Emirates should always be addressed as 'Your Highness' in the first instance, though it is permissible thereafter to say 'Sir'. Similarly, a Ruler, or the President, should in conversation be referred to as 'His Highness'. In Arabic this is '*Sahib as Simu*'. The President of the U.A.E. may be referred to as 'His Highness the President' or, after the first mention, 'The President', or 'Shaikh .....'. Rulers may also, after the first courtesies, be referred to as 'Shaikh .....'. The Amirs of Kuwait, Bahrain and Qatar may be referred to as 'The Amir'.

Crown Princes

The person next to the throne in the monarchical states of Saudi Arabia, Jordan and Morocco is the Crown Prince. He is properly addressed as 'Sir' after the first mention. In the third person he may be referred to as 'His Royal Highness', 'The Crown Prince' or 'Prince .....'.

The Gulf States also have Crown Princes. The rules for addressing them are set out below.

OPENING OF LETTER

'Your Royal Highness' in Saudi Arabia, Jordan and Morocco,
and
'Your Highness' in the Gulf States.

BODY OF LETTER

In the body of the letter 'Your Royal Highness' should generally be used instead of 'you' and 'Your Royal

Highness's' instead of 'your', in the case of Saudi Arabia, Jordan and Morocco. In the Gulf States 'Your Higness' or 'Your Highness's' is used, as in the case of the Rulers themselves.

ENDING OF LETTER

The following forms are possible:
'Finally, Your Royal Highness/Your Highness, I take this opportunity to renew assurances of my highest consideration'
or
'Finally, Your Royal Highness/Your Highness, may I offer my profound respects',
or one of the variations given above as appropriate for Kings, Amirs and Rulers.

ENVELOPE

'His Royal Highness Prince .....
Crown Prince of .....'
or
'His Royal Highness the Crown Prince of .....'
or (in the case of the Gulf States)
'His Highness Shaikh .....
Crown Prince of .....'

Where a Crown Prince also holds other offices, e.g. Deputy Prime Minister and Commander of Armed Forces, these should also be included in the address on the envelope and at the top of the letter itself.

USE OF THE TERM 'HIS ROYAL HIGHNESS' IN SAUDI
ARABIA

In Saudi Arabia all the 'princes of the blood', that is all
the sons and grandsons of His Majesty King Abdul
Aziz ibn Saud, are correctly styled 'His Royal Highness' in the third person and in correspondence these
terms are used in lieu of 'he', 'him', 'his', and 'you'.

Other Princes in Saudi Arabia are styled 'His Highness' and addressed as 'Your Highness'.

However, it is the Arabic version of these titles which
is most frequently used, as it is a requirement in Saudi
Arabia that all official and business correspondence
shall be in Arabic. These titles are '*Sahib as-Simu al
Malaki*' for 'Royal Highness', '*Sahib as-Simu*' for 'Highness'.

USE OF THE TERM 'HIS HIGHNESS' IN OMAN

In Oman the word 'Sayyid' is used invariably for members of the ruling family of Al bu Said and is not used,
as it is in some other parts of Arabia, to denote 'Mister'.

The style 'His Highness' is the prerogative of the
descendants of Sultan Turki and they are addressed in
the third person as 'His Highness Sayyid .....' and in the
second person as 'Your Highness'. 'His Highness' and
'Your Highness' are substituted in correspondence as
appropriate for 'he' and 'him', and for 'you'.

MODE OF ADDRESSING PRINCES AND SHAIKHS WHO
ARE ALSO MINISTERS

Where those bearing the title of His Royal Highness or
His Highness are also Ministers, the correct way of
addressing them is:–

> H.R.H. Prince ..... bin .....
> Minister of .....
> (Address)
> H.H. Shaikh ..... bin .....
> Minister of .....
> (Address)

Presidents

All the other Arab countries except Libya have Presidents, who are directly involved in government as
Heads of State, and protocol is presidential rather
than royal. As in the case of monarchs, it is usual for
correspondence to emanate from or be addressed to
the appropriate official in the President's office.
Advice on this may be sought from the appropriate
Embassy accredited in the country concerned and
other local sources.

In certain cases it may be appropriate to write to the
President direct and in such cases the following forms
of address may be used:

OPENING OF LETTER

'Your Excellency', after which some such phrase as the following may be used:
'May I respectfully present my compliments to Your Excellency and .....'
or
'After Greetings .....'

BODY OF LETTER

In the body of the letter 'Your Excellency' should be regularly used instead of 'you' and 'Your Excellency's' for 'yours'.

ENDING OF LETTER

The following forms or near equivalents are possible:

'Finally, Your Excellency, may I renew assurances of my highest consideration'
or
'Finally, Your Excellency, may I offer my profound respects'.

ENVELOPE

The envelope should be addressed:

> 'His Excellency President .....'
> The Presidential Palace
> .....'

COMMUNICATIONS REFERRING TO THE PRESIDENT

In communications to an official on the Presidential staff, or other official correspondence, the President should be referred to as 'His Excellency' in the body of the letter and 'His Excellency's' should be used instead of 'his'.

ORAL ADDRESS

The President should always be addressed as 'Your Excellency' in the first instance, though he may thereafter be addressed periodically as 'Sir'. Similarly, if one is referring to a President, he should initially be referred to as 'His Excellency' and thereafter 'The President' may be used.

Prime Ministers and Ministers

Prime Ministers, Deputy Prime Ministers and Ministers in Middle Eastern countries are customarily given the honorific of 'His Excellency'. This may apply by local custom to Under-Secretaries of Ministries, though this tends to be by courtesy rather then of right. The following written forms of address may be used:

OPENING OF LETTER

'Your Excellency'
or (less formally, if one knows the Minister)

'Dear (Prime) Minister'
or (if one knows the Minister well)
'Dear Shaikh/Sayyid/Mr .....'

The first form should be followed by an opening such as that used for Presidents. The second and third forms may be followed by less formal openings.

BODY OF LETTER

'Your Excellency' and 'Your Excellency's' should be used judiciously in place of 'you' and 'yours', especially when the most formal method of opening is adopted but this usage may be reduced or dropped when the less formal mode of opening is used.

ENDING OF LETTER

When the most formal mode of writing is adopted, an appropriate ending is:

'Finally, Your Excellency, may I renew assurances of my highest consideration'.
Otherwise, there may be some words conveying respects followed by:
'Yours sincerely'
or
'Yours ever'.

A client of a Ministry may use:
'I have the honour to be,
Sir,
Your Excellency's most obedient servant'

ENVELOPE

The envelope should be addressed as follows:

'His Excellency the Prime Minister'
or
'His Excellency .....'
followed by the Prime Minister's published official address
or (in the case of other Ministers)
'His Excellency the Minister of (e.g. Trade)
or
'His Excellency' (or, where appropriate 'His Royal Highness' or 'His Highness') ..... followed by the published official address.

ORAL ADDRESS

A (Prime) Minister should be addressed initially as 'Your Excellency' but may be addressed subsequently as 'Sir'. 'Your Excellency's' may be judiciously used on occasion instead of 'Yours'. It is also correct to use '(Prime) Minister' as an address.

In the third person, it is correct to refer to the individual office or to 'His Excellency',

e.g. 'The Prime Minister has said .....'
    'His Excellency referred to .....'

There may be exceptions to these rules, where Ministers are members of the ruling family. In such cases, though Ministers may be addressed as above, they may also: be addressed by name, e.g. 'Shaikh Yousef' or 'Sayyid Muhammad' and referred to in the third person in the same vein.

When a Minister bears a Royal or other title, e.g. 'His Royal Highness' or 'His Highness', this is, of course, used instead of 'His Excellency'.

Senior Officials

When a letter is addressed to a senior official with a title such as 'Under-Secretary' or 'Director General' or 'Director' the following forms may be used:

OPENING OF LETTER

Official name and address followed by compliments, e.g.

> '(Full Name)
>> Director General of .....
>>> After compliments may I .....'

or
'Dear .....' (by office, e.g. 'Under-Secretary')
or
'Dear Mr/Shaikh, etc .....'
or (in countries where French is used)
'Monsieur le Directeur, etc).

BODY OF LETTER

There is no particular rule, but any references to Ministers or Royalty should be as suggested above.

END OF LETTER

One of the appropriate forms suggested above as appropriate to Ministers may be used, without the honorific 'Your Excellency' unless this is customary, or (if the 'Dear .....' form is used)
'Yours sincerely'

ENVELOPE

'Mr/Shaikh/Dr/Engineer, etc .....)
followed by the published official address.

ORAL ADDRESS

A senior official may be addressed by his office, e.g. 'Under-Secretary', 'Director General', 'Monsieur le Directeur', etc. or 'Sir' or 'Mr/Shaikh, etc .....'

Military Officers

When a letter is addressed to a senior military officer the same rules generally apply as with senior officials, though it is advisable to enquire about local practice. It is important that they are addressed correctly. In many countries European equivalents, such as General, Colonel, Air Marshal, etc., may be used for oral address and sometimes for correspondence.

Shaikh (or Sheikh)

The title 'Shaikh' is used in rather different ways in the various countries of the Arab world. All these usages derive from the fundamental meaning of the word – a man who is revered for age, wisdom, position, learning or saintliness. The very word 'Shaikh' reveals that in Islam there is no fundamental dichotomy between temporal and spiritual power. A dictionary definition is 'an elderly venerable gentleman; old man; elder; chief; chieftain; patriarch, head of a tribe; title of the ruler of Shaikhdoms in the Gulf; title of scholars trained in the traditional sciences such as clerical dignitaries, members of a religious order, professors of spiritual institutions of higher learning, etc; master; master of an order; senator.'

In the Gulf, the title 'Shaikh' is used not only by the Rulers of the States and the Crown Princes but also by members of Ruling Families and, as elsewhere, the leaders of tribes.

The title 'Shaikh' is often the prerogative of certain families, who have held traditional rule, and such persons may now be found not only in government but also in the private sector. It is important to check on whom it is proper to address in this way. Muslim (*Sharia*) judges (*Kadis*)* and religious leaders are also addressed as 'Shaikh'. A further use is for people who have achieved some distinction in maturity.

The following forms of address are used for 'Shaikhs' who do not hold any higher office, which entitles them to honorifics mentioned previously such as 'His Royal Highness', 'His Highness' and 'His Excellency'.

---

* also spelt *Qadi* or *Qadhi*.

OPENING OF LETTER

'Dear Shaikh (Sheikh, if he uses this form by prefer-
ence) .....'

ENDING OF LETTER

Normal ending as for ordinary correspondence.

ENVELOPE

'Shaikh ..... bin (ibn) .....' 'using where known his pre-
ferred spelling in English),
(where appropriate) Shaikh of ..... (the .....)
(e.g. Tribe).

ORAL ADDRESS

A Shaikh is properly addresses as 'Shaikh .....', though
religious Shaikhs and Minister Judges (*Kadis*) in some
countries, particularly where Turkish influence prevails, as in the Levant, Egypt, Sudan and North Africa,
are usually given Arabic honorifics such as 'Maulana' –
'Our lord'; 'Maulai' – 'My lord' or '*Sidi*' – 'My lord'.
'*Maulana*' and '*Sidi*' are sometimes also used jocularly
as is '*Ya Bey*' in Egypt.

Sayyid (Feminine: Sayyida)

Sayyid traditionally means Lord or Master or a person
respected for birth, personal qualities or fortune. It is
the customary designation of the descendants of Hus-

sain, the younger son of the Prophet Muhammad's daughter, Fatima. Modern usage has applied it to parliamentarians in some countries and in many now it commonly means 'Mister'. This is acceptable in most countries except Oman, where *Sayyid* applies strictly to members of the ruling family. It is used in writing and orally but invariably must be followed by the addressees given name, except in the oral form '*Sayyidi (Sidi)*', 'My lord'.

Sharif (feminine: Sharifa)

This, meaning noble or sublime, is a title accorded to families descended from Hassan, the son of the Prophet Muhammad's daughter Fatima — elder brother to Hussain (see *Sayyid*). Special regard is given to *Sharifs* throughout the Arab world, even though they may be in modest circumstances. Their genealogy is carefully preserved in large Arab towns by the Naqib al Ashraf, the honorary head of the Sharifian families there, and they wear a green turban or a green piece of cloth around the tarbush as a distinguishing mark.

The term is also used for members of the Hashimite family of Jordan. The Grand Sharif of Makkah always enjoyed a particular standing in the Arab world as guardian of the holy places until 1924 when this duty fell upon the family of Al Saud of Saudi Arabia. The Grand Sharif was a dignity established about the middle of the 10th century and became hereditary around 1200 in the House of the Bani Hashim, hence the term Hashemites. Two sons of the Grand Sharif founded new royal Hashemite dynasties in Jordan and Iraq in the 1920s. The latter fell in 1958. The term Hashemite now applies principally to Jordan.

It is important to know precisely who is properly addressed as Sharif. The title is used in writing but not orally. A Hashemite Sharif is normally addressed as 'Sir' but may be addressed as 'Your Highness' on occasion.

Ustadh (in some countries pronounced *Ustaz*)

Ustadh is a title borne by some people of learning, the original meaning being teacher. In some countries it is used as general honorific or as a mode of address to someone with no specific professional qualification.

Professional People

In most Arab countries the customs concerning professional people resemble those of the continental countries more closely than those of the Anglo-Saxon and many Commonwealth countries. Thus the professional qualifications of engineers and lawyers are given specific mention both in writing and oral address and members of a family will often use these qualifications in family and friendly conversations. The following are examples of usage:

OPENING OF LETTER

'Dear Dr ..... (e.g. Muhammad)'
or
'Dear Engineer ..... (e.g. Ahmad)'
or
'Dear Advocate ..... (e.g. Hassan)

BODY OF LETTER

There are no firm rules and the style may be individual both for business and private correspondence. But style should tend towards the more formal, unless one knows the addressee very well.

ENDING OF LETTER

The style of the ending will depend on the style of the letter itself and may be one of the following:

'May I present my respects and good wishes.' 'To you and your wife' may be added when the writer has met the wife socially. But 'your wife' must not be included in Saudi Arabia or other places where tradition is strictly followed
or
'Yours Sincerely'
or
'Yours Ever'

ENVELOPE

People are generally addressed by their profession and full name – with degrees sometimes:

e.g.: 'Engineer Ahmad Rashid'
     'Dr Muhammad Farid (M.D./Ph.D.)'
     'Advocate Hassan Abdullah'
     'Counsellor Rifaat Khalid'
     'Maitre Abdullah Majid'

The terms 'Mister' and 'Monsieur' are also widely used. 'Hajji' or 'Al Hajj' are used for those who have made the pilgrimage.

ORAL ADDRESS

Professional people may, according to usage in particular countries, be addressed in the second person in the following manner:

'Dr Muhammad'
or
'Engineer Ahmad'
or
'Advocate (Maitre) Hassan'
or
'Mister Hamad'
or
'Monsieur Hassan'
or
'Sayyid Hussain'
or
'Sir'
or alternatively merely by their profession, e.g. Engineer, Maitre, Doctor, etc.

Ladies, who have similar professional qualifications in some countries may similarly be addressed in the second person, e.g.:

'Dr Fatima'
or
'Engineer Laila'
or
'Advocate Zainab'.

Ladies without a recognised professional qualification may be addressed as follows:

'Madame Fawzia'
or
'Miss Nura'
or
'Sayyida Aliya'.

Miscellaneous

There tends to be more formality in ordinary speech even with close friends than in Britain and the West and titles are not dropped so readily, though with close friends they need not be used. Consequently references in the third prson are similar to those above. In addition the following may be used as appropriate in second person address:

'Sir'
or
'Madam'
or (often used familiarly in e.g. Jordan and Egypt)
'Abu' (Hassan, etc)
or
'Hajji' (Muhammad) etc.

Though titles have, as we have seen, been formally abolished, Egyptians of some degree of social status commonly refer to each other as, e.g.

Ahmad Bey

Hassan Bey

Ex-Ministers, some of whom may have had particularly distinguished careers (enquiries are desirable as to local form) are sometimes still addressed as 'Your Excellency', etc, but may also be addressed as 'Mr .....' or merely 'Sir'.

In Egypt too, taxi drivers, hotel servants, etc. may address a male visitor as *'Ya Bey'*, *'Ya Basha'* *'Ya Khawaja'* and a female as *'Ya Sitt'*. These are terms of respect, traditionally and habitually used to people of higher social status, even in a much more egalitarian era, amongst and by Egyptians themselves. *'Khawaja'* applies only to foreigners and its use may imply an intention to do an advantageous bargain of some sort with you!

Names in the Arab World

The usual custom in the Middle East is for a man or woman to have his or her 'given' name followed by that of the father and grandfather, e.g.

> *Ahmad bin Muhammad bin Hassan*. The classical word for son is *'ibn'* but *'bin'* is widely used particularly in the Arabian Peninsula. Another variation is *'wad'* or *'walad'* (spelt *'ould'* in the

Maghrab countries). In some countries the '*bin*' is omitted and so the name is written simply as *Ahmad Muhammad Hassan*.

Fatima bint Hussain bin Abdulla. '*Bint*' means 'daughter of' or 'a girl'.

This explains why some Middle Eastern countries have on their immigration forms 'Name ..... Father's Name ..... Grandfather's Name .....'

Ahmad would normally be addressed as 'Mr Ahmad' in short both in writing and orally. There can be no question of calling him 'Mr Muhammad' or 'Mr Hassan', unless he has indicated a desire for this, e.g. by putting 'Mr A.M. Hassan' on his own card or notepaper.

However, in some cases people in the Middle East have adopted a family name, bearing some resemblance to a surname, and this is, as in the case of European surnames, often attributable to an office held or a trade plied by a forebear or to his place of origin. In such cases the person may be addressed as 'Mr (whatever the family name is)'.

For example:–

Ahmad Muhammad al *Qaraquli* (the custodian) – Mr Qaraquli
Ahmad Muhammad al *Jazzar* (the butcher) – Mr Jazzar
Ahmad Muhammad al *Maghrabi* (the Maghrabi, i.e. coming from North West Africa) – Mr al Maghrabi
Ahmad Muhammad al *Tounsi* (the Tunisian – Mr Tounsi
Ahmad Muhammad *Tantawi* (from Tanta) – Mr Tantawi

It is not wrong to address such persons as Mr Ahmad but, if one learns that he prefers to be known by his family name, it should be used. The use of family names is increasing.

In countries where it is more usual to adopt family names, there is no great difficulty about addressing the wife, if, for example, one wishes to write a 'thank-you' letter for entertainment offered. She may be addressed as e.g.

Mrs Qaraquli, Mrs Jazzar, etc.

This, of course, presupposes that the lady in question moves in mixed society, as is likely in some countries. If, however, the husband has some such name only as 'Ahmad Muhammad Hassan', i.e. not a family name, but at the same time has a wife who moves in mixed society, one must enquire how she is properly addressed. There are several possibilities:

By her own name, if one knows her well enough, in the body of the letter e.g. 'Dear Laila'. Even then one would need to enquire how to address the envelope, which might take either of the following forms:
'*Mrs Ahmad Muhammad Hassan*' or
'*Mrs Ahmad*' or, possibly, she might like to be known as '*Mrs Hassan*', even though the grandfather's name is not a descriptive family name.

Transliteration of names – and generally

Owing to the vagaries of style, habit and scholarship, the same Arab name may be spelt differently in different parts of the Arab world. This caused T.E. Lawrence (perhaps in despair of finding any overall logical basis for easy transliteration, though there are plenty of real scholars and of pedants to offer their views!) to adopt a very cavalier attitude to it. In the preface to *Seven Pillars of Wisdom* by A.W. Lawrence, T.E.'s brother, there are given a number of questions by the publisher with the author's answers, including:

Q.	A.
attach a list of queries raised by F who is reading the proofs. He finds these very clean, but full of inconsistencies in the spelling of proper names, a point which reviewers often take up. Will you annotate it in the margin so that I can get the proofs straightened?	Annotated: not very helpfully perhaps. Arabic names won't go into English, exactly, for their consonants are not the same as ours, and their vowels, like ours, vary from district to district. There are some 'scientific' systems of transliteration, helpful to people who know enough Arabic not to need helping, but a wash-out for the world.
Slip 78. Sherif Abd el Mayin of slip 68 becomes el Main, el Mayein, al Muein, el Mayin, and el Muein.	Good egg. I call this really ingenious.

People in the Middle East usually have their own view on how their names should be transliterated and prefer one usage to another. Sometimes this depends on whether the country has a tradition of British or French influence. For example 'Shorbagy' and 'Chourbagui' are the same word in Arabic, but one has been transliterated according to the English tradition and the other according to the French. Thus 'Mohamed', 'Muhammad', 'Muhamad' and 'Mahmet' are all versions of the same Arab name.

The only safe rules, therefore, are:—

First, follow the general custom of transliteration of the particular country.
Secondly, find out how anyone addressed prefers his name to be spelt.

Diplomatic

Ambassadors are appointed by their respective Heads of State and on arrival in the state to which they are accredited present their 'credentials' to the Head of that State. They are representatives of their country and the following forms of address are appropriate:

OPENING OF LETTER

The method of address depends on the nature of the communication and the degree of its formality, but the following are on different occasions appropriate:

'Your Excellency'
'My Dear/Dear Ambassador'
'Dear Mr Ambassador' (appropriate only for U.S. Ambassadors or those who follow U.S. custom)
'Dear Mr/Monsieur/Herr/Dr .....'

BODY OF LETTER

There is no specific rule for this, but where the very formal style of address is used, 'Your Excellency' and 'Your Excellency's' may be used for 'you' and 'yours', but this should not be laboured particularly in the case of ambassadors of countries such as the Anglo-Saxons and Scandinavians, where this style is not habitually used in their home countries.

ENDING OF LETTER

'Finally, Your Excellency, I take this opportunity to renew assurances of my highest consideration'
'Please accept, Your Excellency, my respectful compliments'
'Yours sincerely/faithfully'

ENVELOPE

The envelope should be addressed:

'His Excellency Mr/Monsieur/Dr/Herr, etc. .....'
    ..... Embassy
    or 'Embassy of .....'
        ..... (actual address if appropriate)
            ..... (capital)

Where an envelope is addressed to an ambassador and an ambassadress at the same time, the following are possible:

'Their Excellencies Monsieur and Madame/Mr and Mrs/etc. .....'
(used in the case of countries adopting contiental custom)

followed by the address as above.

'His Excellency the Ambassador of ..... and Madame/ Mrs .....'

followed by actual address and name of capital as above.

ORAL ADDRESS

The following are correct according to circumstances:

'Your Excellency'
'Excellency'
'Sir'
'Mr Ambassador' – where U.S. usage is adopted.

It is customary in British Embassies for the staff to address the Ambassador as 'Sir', though Christian names are used between all other members of his staff, whether senior or junior. A British visitor may call the Ambassador 'Sir', unless he knows him well personally. Other members of the staff may be addressed as 'Mr .....' until Christian name terms are established.

Some other countries' Embassies tend to be more formal and use the terms 'Your Excellency' and 'Excellency' much more freely.

British Ambassadors are not addressed as 'Your Excellency' after relinquishing their appointments, but in the case of many other countries retired Ambassadors retain their title of Ambassador and the style of 'Excellency'. Retired U.S. Ambassadors also customarily retain their titles of 'Ambassador' or 'Mr Ambassador'.

Chargés d'Affaires and Consuls-General are not customarily entitled to the address 'His/Your Excellency'.

Chapter 4

Correspondence

General

Arabic is the language used for official, business and social purposes all over the Middle East, though English and, in some countries, French, especially in North Africa, Egypt, Lebanon and Syria, are used to a varying extent. Arabic is the only language used in Saudi Arabia for official correspondence and all communications by letter to Ministries and Government agencies must be in that language. An exception is at present made for telexes for official business purposes.

Official Correspondence

Suitable openings and terminations are suggested in Chapter 3 'Modes of Address'. The body of the letter will naturally depend on circumstances. But it is necessary to be polite as well as clear and care should be taken not to include phrases which might unintentionally cause offence. Advice on tricky points can be taken locally and Embassies may also be asked to advise where necessary.

Business Letters

Here the same rules apply as to business correspondence in Western countries, though it is obviously more important to make sure that an unnecessarily offending phrase is not included as in the case of official correspondence.

Letters of Congratulation

It is usual to send letters of congratulation to close friends on marriage, the birth of a child or on a promotion. The style should be individual but can be quite fulsome. If one is sending a letter in Arabic it should be prepared by a local Arab. The following are suitable matters for inclusion:

MARRIAGE

Congratulations – general
Hope that the marriage may be blessed
Hope for prosperity and children

BIRTH OF A CHILD
(As in other parts of the East, a father is customarily more delighted by a son than a daughter)

Congratulations
Happiness
Hope that the next child may be a boy (where appropriate, though some Arab families nowadays feel less strongly on this).

PROMOTION

Congratulations
Hope that the recipient may reach the highest office
(even a little exaggerated hope is not out of place).

Letters of Condolence

Letters of condolence to close friends or particular
contacts are appropriate. The following thoughts, re-
flecting Arabic phrases commonly used, may be included:

> Hope that God may grant solace
> Eternity and existence are God's
> We all belong to God and are returning to Him.

'Thank You' Letters

It is polite to write a letter of thanks if one has been
entertained personally by a Minister, a senior official
or other eminent personage and sometimes merely if
one has been received by such a person. There is no
need, however, to write if one has been only one of
many guests at a large gathering.

In cities such as Cairo, Beirut and Baghdad, European custom about writing letters of thanks after
receiving hospitality, whether for a meal or otherwise,
is generally followed. A short note of thanks to one's
hostess never goes amiss. Flowers may be sent at the
same time, though it is customary sometimes to send
them in advance or to arrive with them. Local enquiry
should be made as to the practice.

Invitations

LANGUAGE

Invitations may, in differnt countries, be printed in Arabic, a combination of Arabic and English or Arabic and French. Sometimes one version is printed on one side of the card and one on the other and sometimes invitations are only in English or French.

CARDS – RECEIPT OF INVITATION

Cards of invitation to a meal, may, in some countries, be distributed to a very large number of people and, when this happens, there is often no R.S.V.P. In such cases one may expect an enormous gathering with free seating. In the case of such invitations there is no need to reply, unless one wishes to make a particular point of excusing oneself for some reason. It is then appropriate to speak or write to the Private Secretary, or similar aide, of the person issuing the invitation. In other cases, one naturally should reply to an invitation.

CARDS – ISSUING INVITATIONS

The form of an invitation can be the same as elsewhere. A suitable wording for a special function would be:

> On the occasion of ..... (the visit of the Chairman of .....)
>
> ....
>
> has the honour to request the presence of
>
> ....

at ..... (a Luncheon/Buffet Supper)
on the ..... of ..... at ..... (a.m./p.m.)
R.S.V.P.
..... (address)
..... (telephone)

If one issues an invitation with R.S.V.P. on it, it does not follow that all the invited guests will reply, for these letters do not carry great compulsion in the Middle East, perhaps because of the open and generous approach to hospitality which applies generally. This should not dispirit one, for they may yet come. But it is hard to know, sometimes, how many people will actually turn up at a cocktail party or buffet dinner. 'Card drill' is not very closely followed and people are generally not very formal over this, though there are exceptions. If the invitation is for a small sit-down dinner and answers have not been received, it is wise to telephone the Secretary of the people invited and gently ask if they are coming.

If one wishes to invite a Minister or a person of considerable standing, it is best to specify the particular reason why he or she has been invited. For instance, for a large party the card may carry some such words written on the top as 'To meet/or In Honour of .....' But if the party is smaller and one particularly wants the local personage to attend, it is best to ring the Private Secretary first and explain the occasion of the invitation.

In some cases it is tactful to write a personal letter to the person concerned to explain the nature of the occasion – for example, a lunch on the occasion of the visit of the Chairman of a company, or a distinguished person who is well known for something special or has a special connection with the particular country.

Visiting and Business Cards

Old customs about use of visiting cards have all but died, although they are preserved a little in diplomatic circles. In general, however, nowadays people use their visiting cards more as business cards and it is not uncommon to exchange these with senior officials and sometimes Ministers. It is neither wise nor polite, however, to thrust such cards on Ministers unless one has first established that this is acceptable practice in the particular country concerned. There need not, however, be the same inhibition about offering cards to officials down the line.

Most Arab businessmen have business cards in Arabic. They also often have them in English and French. Sometimes cards are in Arabic on one side and English or French on the other. There is some advantage for a foreign businessman in having such dual-language cards.

Chapter 5

Entertaining

General

Although there is a similarity between formal banquets in any part of the Middle East, the manner of informal entertaining differs quite widely. It is, however, the general tradition in the Arab world to be very liberal with food and far more is usually provided than can be consumed by the actual guests. Nothing is wasted in the long run as, particularly after the largest meals in the traditional style, all the unconsumed food is eaten by members of the family, retainers, drivers and others who are not present at the function itself.

Traditional Arab hospitality is not only liberal but is provided without regard for rank or class for all those invited, together with their staff, retinue or servants, though the guests of honour sit in the highest places.

Entertainment to which one may be invited

One may be invited to:

> *Formal entertainment,* which may be a traditional style lunch or dinner or more likely a modern modification of it in parts of Arabia, notably the Arabian Peninsula.

or
a Buffet reception
or
a Reception with drinks and light refreshments
to eat
or
a European style meal;

Informal Entertainment, which may take the form
of:
a private lunch or dinner either at home or in a
restaurant,
or
a private buffet lunch or dinner (a very popular
form of entertainment)
or
a cocktail party
or
a tea party

Traditional lunches and dinners and modern modifications

The Arab tradition, which perhaps has its origins in
Bedu life, is to eat out of a large common bowl often
surrounded by a number of side dishes, though where
the numbers are too large to sit round a single communal tray, a series of similar sets are put out in a row.
Traditionally people eat sitting or half-kneeling on the
ground, the dishes of food being set out on a cloth or
mat. Food was traditionally eaten with the right hand
and not with knife, fork and spoon. Other customs
concerning traditional entertaining and misapprehen-

sions about them, such as being offered the sheep's eye, are dealt with in Appendix E.

Most formal entertaining nowadays is to some extent an adaptation of the old style and large official gatherings in Saudi Arabia and the Arabian Peninsula combine features of the old and new worlds, but everywhere now there are likely to be tables and chairs. Coffee is likely to be served in the Arabian style before the meal in a *majlis* or outer room. One will be then invited to the dining room with the word *'Tafaddal'* — which really means 'be pleased to' or 'be good as to .....' do something, for example, proceed to the table, start eating or precede another. There are few lunches or dinners given by hosts in the Arab world where there is a formal placement at tables, though sometimes seats are allocated at a high table, and possibly other prominent tables, for V.I.Ps. More often there is free seating at such functions for the majority.

The places at table are likely to be set in European style with knives, forks, spoons and plates, but the dishes set out on the table will usually be traditional Arab ones, such as piled rice, a whole sheep or goat, some fish dish and a variety of side dishes. Though one's plate may well be heaped by one's host or neighbour with far more food than one can manage, it is not obligatory to eat it all, even if chided gently for lack of appetite with some such phrase as 'But you have not eaten'. Some Arab foods are mentioned in Appendix G.

A very large formal gathering in Iraq, Jordan, Syria or parts of North Africa may take this form but elsewhere, for example, in Egypt, Sudan and Lebanon smaller dishes may be provided and the whole sheep or goat is less often displayed.

Buffet Receptions

The hosts (and, in some countries, hostesses) and guests of honour on such occasions stand at the entrance of the reception room to greet and shake hands with their guests. Shortly after arrival drinks, either soft or alcoholic, are served. A buffet may be ready to be eaten immediately or sometimes it may be brought later and be in a separate room.

The dishes are likely to be varied and considerable in number. Knives and forks are usually provided but sometimes there are 'finger eats'.

At some parties the hosts (and hostess) may stand to say goodbye to their guests, but it is far more usual for people to come and go on such occasions very freely. It is quite acceptable at many such functions to look in for a very short time.

European style Lunches and Dinners

There is little to be said about these as European custom is basically followed, though general considerations about manners and alcohol need to be kept in mind.

Informal Entertainment

If one is invited to informal entertainment such as a lunch or a dinner party by an Arab one will do well to take cues from others and thus avoid putting a foot wrong. Customs differ considerably.

Women

The old custom through the Arab and Muslim world was that there was no mixed entertaining; men only entertained men and women only women. This still applies throughout most of the region and it remains the general rule at most levels of society in all the countries.

None the less, most of the major cities have considerable numbers of men and women who have a modern education and see no inconsistency between mixed social contact and Islam. In several countries, e.g. Egypt and Iraq, women play a prominent part in Government and public affairs and hold ministerial and high official positions. In other countries this would be unthinkable.

Consequently among many such people, especially in cities like Cairo and Baghdad, mixed dinners, lunches and cocktail parties are frequent and normal. Many of the people a foreigner is likely to meet entertain in this way. On the other hand in other areas, such as much of the Gulf and Saudi Arabia, a foreigner is more likely to be entertained, or to offer entertainment, at an entirely male party.

When parties are mixed, the men and women still have a tendency to segregate, but conversation with the ladies is free and can often be very lively. Among topics of conversation family and family affairs as well as politics and public affairs often feature.

Dress

Dress nowadays for any sort of formal entertaining for European men is virtually always a dark lounge suit.

European ladies may have to enquire about suitable wear for a particular function.

Punctuality

Punctuality is a tricky question. On formal occasions it is, of course, necessary to be punctual and embarrassment can easily be caused if one is not. However, there is much greater flexibility in respect of less formal entertaining and the habit of the Middle East is for parties to start rather late, even if the starting time of the invitation is stated to be relatively early.

The Middle East custom is often to serve dinner very late, particularly at private parties, and there may be considerable drinking time before the meal arrives. On one occasion a British guest was invited with his wife to a small party and arrived on time, regarding the invitation as of a somewhat formal nature. As the occasion was a celebration, they drank champagne from 8.00 p.m. sharp until after midnight, when the meal was served. However, parties may break up quite abruptly immediately after coffee has been served following a meal.

It is wise to enquire about the style of entertaining one may encounter in any particular country. Likewise, it is wise to enquire what form of entertainment local people prefer if one is to issue an invitation. On the whole people in the Middle East prefer buffets to a formal dinner and guests are liable to arrive up to an hour and a half late, unless one makes it plain that the occasion is a sit-down affair timed for a certain hour.

Alcohol

Alcohol is a difficult subject because of differences in the strictness with which the Koran is interpreted. In some countries, for example Saudi Arabia and Kuwait, prohibition of alcohol is total and will not in any circumstances be served. It may well not be served at large gatherings in some other Arab countries, particularly in the Gulf area, though at smaller functions it may well be. Some countries, for example Egypt, Iraq, the Lebanon, Syria and some North African countries follow a more relaxed practice. Some countries have their own vineyards. The only good advice about drinking is to follow the custom of one's hosts – without comment!

Smoking

At some parties there is no smoking; at others there is. If one wishes to smoke, one should observe what other people are doing and perhaps ask about local custom. It is not wise to assume that lighting up will give no offence.

Table Manners

These are very similar at sit-down functions to those in Europe and the U.S.A. except that, where the occasion is a modern modification of traditional style entertaining, one will help oneself from the numerous dishes placed on the table. Sometimes one's host or neighbour will also assist and press food on one. Knives, forks and spoons are used.

Toothpicks are often provided at formal and informal functions and may, if required, be used quite freely and openly, the picking operating being judiciously shielded by the other hand.

Thanks after a Meal

Immediately after a meal one may say to one's host or hostess 'Sufra Daima', as a gesture of thanks. It means 'May your table always be spread'.

Flowers and small presents

In some countries it is customary to send flowers to one's hostess either before or after a party or to take a small present. Enquiry about local custom is advisable.

Coffee and Tea

In the Arabian peninsula, coffee is not merely a drink, it is a ceremony and, in certain less urban parts, if one is invited to drink coffee a small repast may be served with it. The coffee itself is bitter and is frequently laced with cardamom or other spices for additional flavour. It is traditionally served in a small round cup by a servant with a deep flourish after he has poured it individually from a silver, copper or brass coffee pot – or even a Thermos flask. The cup is liable to be filled again and again until one shakes it with a degree of vigour from side to side by rocking the wrist. An assiduous servant may still, after a clear signal, press yet another cup on one, but the process can be terminated by a still more vigorous movement and a shake of the head on the next occasion.

Where 'Turkish coffee' is drunk – and this is very common in offices in the more northern areas of the Middle East as well as Egypt and the Sudan – one may be asked how one likes one's coffee. There are three gradations; first '*mazbut*' (literally 'correct') with medium sugar; secondly '*ziada*' literally 'more') with heavy sugaring; and '*sada*' (literally 'plain') without any sugar at all. This form of coffee is served with a glass of cold water, usually drunk before the coffee, and the ceremonial of the peninsula does not prevail.

One may frequently be asked whether one wishes coffee or tea. Tea is normally served in one of two ways: either with a rich amount of milk and sugar, which may not be entirely to European taste, or clear without milk but with sugar. In Iraq and some Gulf States one may be offered '*shai hamudh*' (bitter tea) which is a refreshing and piquant brew made from dried limes imported from the coast of Oman.

Tea Parties

There is little to be said about these, except that one may be given a great quantity of cakes on the same plate. It is not necessary to eat them all, but merely to do some justice to them.

Offering Entertainment

One may, according to circumstances, offer any of the common forms of formal or informal entertainment applying in the Middle East.

By and large people in the Middle East prefer buffet lunches or dinners, which gives them some flexibility about the timing of arrival and departure. This is, therefore, often the best solution.

If entertaining a Minister or some very senior person in the Middle East, the considerations set out in Chapter 6 on Precedence and Protocol should be borne in mind, especially in connection with meeting, greeting and seeing off.

If uncertain whether to make the party a mixed one or not, or whether a man's wife is likely to accept an invitation, it is best to enquire. It is also useful to obtain some idea of a guest's tastes about forms of entertainment and it is best to enquire whether it is advisable to offer alcohol or not. Pork and bacon must in no circumstances be offered to Muslims.

Wedding Invitations

One may be invited to a party or a series of parties to celebrate a wedding. Information on the nature of a Muslim wedding is given in Appendix F. In Arabia and the stricter areas, there will be separate events for men and women and normally only women will meet the bride and female members of the families. In the large cities, however, the parties will normally be mixed.

One example of an invitation is:

In the name of God the Merciful the Compassionate

....

request/s the pleasure of your company on the
occasion of the wedding of

....

with the daughter of

....

at .... on ....

In Arabia and the stricter areas the bride will not usually be named, whereas she would probably be elsewhere, for example in the large cities.

The form of reply to an invitation will be dictated by the wording of the card and by the particular circumstances.

If one is invited to a wedding where the celebrations span several days or comprise various events, one will usually have guidance on timing, transport, dress and behaviour from a special person appointed to look after guests as well as from the written communications.

It is usual to give presents for weddings and these may be handed over, or left in an appropriate place, at the wedding reception when this is obviously the main event. If in doubt, it is best to ask how to deliver presents.

It is often very difficult to know what to give as a wedding present, particularly to those who are very wealthy. It is best to look for something individual, which might be of particular interest to the recipients.

Chapter 6

Precedence and Protocol

Rules of precedence and protocol vary from country to country and there are obviously differences between the Monarchies and Gulf Emirates on the one hand and the Presidential Republics on the other.

Precedence List

The precedence in some countries is set out in a Precedence List, kept by the Royal or Presidential Protocol and the Protocol Department of the Ministry of Foreign Affairs. However, if there is no published precedence list, matters of precedence are settled by custom and practice and local enquiry may be necessary.

Precedence in Monarchical Countries

The normal precedence in monarchical countries is:

>   The King, Sultan, Amir or Ruler
>   Immediate members of the Ruling Family, including Crown Princes, in their own established order
>   Ministers

Ambassadors of foreign countries accredited
Deputy Ministers
Commanders of Armed Forces
Permanent Under-Secretaries or Secretaries-
  General of Ministries
Other senior officers and officials, religious
  leaders and academics such as Vice-Chancellor
Distinguished civilians including senior mem-
  bers of foreign business communities

Where there is a formal line-up, for example at an air-port to welcome a visiting Head of State, a senior Protocol Officer will be in charge and, following the local practice, will line everyone up in the proper order.

Precedence in Presidential States

In Presidential states the general order of precedence is:

The President
The Prime Minister (if there is one)
Ministers
Ambassadors of foreign countries accredited
Deputy Ministers
Commanders of Armed Forces
Permanent Under-Secretaries or Secretaries-
  General of Ministries
Other senior officers and officials, religious
  leaders and senior academics such as Vice-
  Chancellors
Distinguished civilians including members of
  the foreign business communities

The position of religious leaders, such as Grand Kadi or Mufti, may vary from country to country as may the precise precedence accorded to Service Commanders.

Relevance of Precedence

Precedence is of relevance at formal and official functions, but such occasions pose no problem for a foreigner as the authorities of the State deal with this.

For the foreigner, precedence is of relevance when he, or the body he is representing, holds a function which may involve several local people of rank. In such cases precise knowledge of relative precedence in the particular country becomes important.

Titles

There are no titles any longer in the Middle East other than those borne by Royalty and those of Sayyid, Sharif and Shaikh (also see Modes of Address). Military rank in translation follow the Western style, for example, General, Brigadier, Colonel, etc.

Decorations

In some countries, such as Jordan, Oman and Morocco, decorations and orders are conferred by the Head of State. It is helpful to know something of these and their relative importance. Advice should be taken locally as to whether these decorations are much used and, if so, whether they should be included on invitations, etc. The general rule is that they are not usually written.

If a local person has been awarded a British decoration, it is polite to know of this and to make suitable mention of it.

Protocol and Behaviour at Official Functions

An invitation to an official function will usually specify such matters as:

> dress and whether orders and decorations are to be worn
>
> arrangements for setting down (including provision of special car stickers)
>
> arrangements for parking
>
> time of arrival – but it may often be wise to enquire whether this means arrival before a particular time or between certain times. Invitations are not always entirely clear on this.

It is advisable when an invitation in Arabic is received to have it translated in full so that one is fully aware of all the implications.

An official guest of a monarch or of a government will, however, be placed in charge of a Protocol officer, whose duty includes guiding the guest in all matters of protocol, address, behaviour and precedence.

On other formal occasions, whatever the local rules of precedence and protocol, all those attending will be told what to do or directed to seats allocated, if they have received official invitations.

Audiences

If one is granted an audience by a sovereign, including the Amirs and Rulers in the Gulf, one will be told where this will be held and at what time. On arrival, an official will meet one and, perhaps after a short spell in a waiting room, conduct one to the audience. After initial greetings (See Chapter 3 Modes of Address), there will be an exchange of pleasantries before any business is conducted. The old custom was that no mention of business was ever made until coffee had been drunk.

Gulf States

In the Gulf States, the Amirs and Shaikhs and their people still follow ancient Arab custom over social approaches. This is a mixture of tradition and informality, but there are unwritten rules and advice is necessary locally on how, if and when to approach a Shaikh on a great occasion.

When an approach is appropriate, hands are shaken and brief greetings exchanged. The custom among men close to one another in blood or friendship is to exchange kisses on the nose, but there is no need to emulate them as one would a hug in the Northern Arab world.

Meeting with Presidents

Very much the same procedure is followed as in the case of audiences.

Meetings with Ministers and Senior Officials

When one calls on a Minister by appointment, there is usually no special formality. One goes to the relevant ministry, where one will be shown to the office of the Minister's Private Secretary. After greetings, there will be an exchange of pleasantries before business is started. It is polite sometimes to approach the specific subject of business somewhat obliquely in the first instance. One should be careful not to take up too much of the Minister's time.

Traditionally in the Arab world a man's status determined how far his host accompanied him on his onward journey. There is sometimes a dim reflection of this practice after a call, when occasionally the man giving the appointment will accompany you to the car, or to an outer door or a lift. However, the general custom is that farewells are said in the office and, if anyone accompanies one further, it is usually a junior or a secretary.

Protocol towards Senior Local Personages

If entertaining a senior personage, such as a Minister, Deputy Minister, senior official, e.g. at the opening of some project, at a large reception in an hotel or at home, it is important to find out about local custom and protocol as well as precedence. Sources of information are:

> one's own Embassy
> one's business associate or agent

local friends
the private secretary to a Minister or senior
   official or the A.D.C. to senior officer.

Where there is a distinguished guest, it is important
that other guests are introduced to him in such a
manner that everyone involved is clearly informed of
the name and business of the other. Skill in intro-
ductions is an important asset. In effecting such intro-
ductions, and indeed in general conversation, it is wise
to bear in mind the considerations set out in Chapter 3
'Mode of Address'.

If one has a particularly distinguished visitor to call
or a Minister or very senior person to dinner, lunch or
a reception, one should accompany him to his car or, if
circumstances make this too difficult, ensure that
someone of adequate seniority accompanies him.

If the occasion is a reception, cocktail party or buffet
dinner, there is obviously greater informality. Such
occasions are consequently in many ways easier and indeed nowadays more usual. It is important, however,
that the host greets any Minister who attends the
occasion and that he sees him off. He may also invite
his own Ambassador to play some suitable and special
role *vis à vis* the Minister or Ministers.

Protocol towards Members of Armed Forces

A very senior officer of the Armed Forces or the Police
is entitled to special courtesies if invited to attend a
party, but it is advisable to enquire locally how he and

his wife rate *vis à vis* other distinguished guests from the same country and recourse may again be had to the precedence list, if available. In general, the top-ranking officers usually rank after the Deputy Ministers, who, unlike full Ministers, come after foreign Ambassadors. However, the position is obviously different if the officers also hold ministerial rank.

Ambassadors and Local Personages

Ambassadors of foreign countries accredited normally rank with, but after, Ministers, but if inviting one's own Ambassador to attend a private occasion, such as an opening ceremony, he may be invited to help greet and entertain a local minister or dignitary. Very often it would be appropriate, for instance, to seat them side by side on such an occasion.

In deciding *placement* at a formal dinner or on a platform, one's own Ambassador would be expected by Ministers and officials of the host country to have proper place. It is often best to place the Ambassador at one end of a dinner table and in some cases Ambassadors and Ambassadresses are asked to help act partly as official hosts to Ministers or distinguished guests and their wives.

Where there are doubts about the relative seniority of local notables, it is easier and safer to have a cocktail party, a reception or a buffet dinner. (Also see Chapter 5 'Entertaining'). Nevertheless the very small intimate dinner party either at home or in a restaurant also has a place.

Precedence amongst Ambassadors

Ambassadors take their relative precedence in any country to which they are accredited strictly in accordance with the date on which they presented their credentials. This is always shown in the locally published Diplomatic List published by the Ministry of Foreign Affairs. The size of the respective Embassies or other factors are in no way relevant in this respect. This relative precedence can be of direct relevance if entertaining ambassadors from more than one country at the same time. On such occasions one's own Ambassador may be asked to play some special role such as that suggested above.

Consuls-General and Consuls

Where there is a Consul-General or Consul in a town, other than the capital where the Embassy is situated, he, as the 'flag-bearer', is treated as the senior national. In capitals where the Ambassador resides the Consul General or Consul still has a special responsibility for the community and this is normally recognized though he ranks officially after those senior to him on an Embassy list.

Diplomatic Embassy Staff

If in contact with Embassy Officials, it is advisable to be aware of the Diplomatic ranks:

Ambassador
Minister (sometimes Minister/Counsellor)
Counsellor
First Secretary
Second Secretary
Third Secretary
Attaché

Where there is more than one holding a particular rank, seniority is in accordance with that shown on the official Embassy list. Sometimes particular ranks also have designations, e.g. First Secretary (Commercial) or Counsellor (Economic). In addition to the civilian diplomatic staff, most Embassies have Service Attachés, e.g. Military Attaché, Naval Attaché and Air Attaché. The senior of these nowadays, at least in British Embassies, is called the Defence Attaché. Their relative precedence is also shown in the Diplomatic List.

Expatriate Community

There are no set rules for precedence among members of the local expatriate community but, by custom, senior bankers and very senior professional people often have a special position. Age, length of service and prominence in local activities are also relevant.

Chapter 7

Manners and General Behaviour

Manners Generally

Manners, as we have seen, are of great importance in the Middle East and much attention is devoted to them, particularly in bringing up children. The concept of respect has not disappeared and modes of address (see Chapter 3) illustrate the importance still attached to consideration for others.

Children and Parents

A child's sense of duty and respect towards parents is very marked and this continues right through to old age. Family ties remain strong and children tend not to break away, but to retain homing habits. A man may well see, or speak on the telephone to, each of his grown up and professional children every day. The family unit is the basis of society and the bond of social stability, and children generally tend to respect parents, teachers and older people in a manner formerly more common than now in the West.

Traditionally children tended to be small models of grown-ups. However, though importance is still given to manners, they are often nowadays allowed indulgences such as staying up very late with their parents as with many continental children.

Women

Some mention of the place of women in Middle Eastern life is made in Chapters 1 and 6 but a little more should be said. All Arab women give great attention to their children, whether they keep to the harim or lead an active public life or spend most of their time as a housewife in cities where society at some levels is open and mixed.

The fact that women in some parts of Arabia are veiled and do not customarily move in mixed society should not conceal the degree of their influence. Monarchs, Rulers, Statesmen, merchants and men from many walks of life have always been in the habit not only of paying great deference to their mothers and wives but also of consulting them on many matters. Their influence may be discreet but can be very great and quite as effective as the influence of Western women on their menfolk.

In some parts of Arabia women do not move in mixed society at all and consequently a man will not normally meet them. In such places, where the rules of traditional society prevail, a man should not normally make specific enquiries about the wife or daughters, though it is polite to ask after the health of the 'family' or 'the children'. There can, however, be exceptions and gradation in this regard. Women visitors are frequently invited to meet a host's wife and daughters and occasionally, a man might be specially invited to pay a short visit to them. But customs vary from place to place and between families.

Where women do move in mixed society, there are slight differences between customs in Europe and the U.S.A. and the Middle East. For instance if a foreign man is greeting a friend and his wife from the Middle East he would normally greet and shake hands with the man first. There is thus a small implied seeking of permission to address the wife. If one goes to a party where there is dancing, it may be polite and advisable to ask the husband before inviting the lady to dance.

Nature of Greetings and Communication

There tends to be genuineness in human communication, even where this is of a rough or earthy kind, and old customs still prevail. Customary phrases, often with religious overtones, are given in the list of Arabic phrases on p. 000. Greeting is of an older world flavour and the now customary phrase in Britain and parts of the West, 'Hallo', by itself would not be generally acceptable, except amongst some of the young, as implying a degree of disrespect.

Some junior officials in the Middle East are not, it is true, always as polite as their Western counterparts, but press, television and radio interviewers show far greater politeness and less aggression towards Ministers and other personalities interviewed. Moreover, they would never drop a man's rank and refer to him as 'John Smith'. The prefix Shaikh, Doctor, Mister, Monsieur, etc. would not be dropped, for in common parlance, at home as well as in public, they will frequently refer to 'His Excellency the Minister' or 'His Excellency'.

Thanks for Small Services

While manners are generally more demonstrative in the Middle East than in the West, there is one major exception and that is that, though thanks may be very profuse on occasion among the most sophisticated town dwellers, they are generally not, where older custom prevails, conveyed for formal gifts, nor is it usual to thank someone for some small service, e.g. picking up a handkerchief. Such a trifling service is taken for granted on the basis that either would do the same for the other without thinking anything of it.

However, this custom has already changed in towns and the Western custom is increasingly followed.

Shaking Hands

There is a great deal of shaking of hands in the Middle East and it is the invariable custom for men to shake hands on greeting, always with the right hand. One may shake hands with the same person several times in the course of the day and in some countries it is the custom to shake hands repeatedly on greeting with the words pronounced equally often 'Kaif Halak' – 'How are you?'. A tip formerly given to British officials going to the Middle East was 'When in doubt, shake hands'. One, of course, shakes hands with emancipated and sophisticated women in some parts of the Middle East, but a man should not shake hands with women in areas where strict Muslim custom is followed unless the woman herself shows an inclination to do so. A woman, according to some of the strictest Muslims, should touch no man other than her husband.

Kissing

In the Arabian Peninsula close male members of a family kiss each other on the nose, especially in Shaikhly families, and subjects kiss Shaikhs on the nose as a sign of respect. One should not normally follow their example. However, it is a different matter in Middle East countries which have adopted Continental custom, and one may embrace and kiss male friends in the Continental manner. Reciprocate without shunning if approached in this way. In some such countries one may sometimes greet wives and daughters of friends in the Continental manner with a kiss on both cheeks, but equally one should not assume that this would be acceptable until a very close friendship is established and then only on private occasions.

In general there is not the same aversion to, or phobia about, physical contact between males as is displayed by the Anglo-Saxons and males in the Middle East frequently hold hands quite innocently as well as embracing. From time to time the visitor may have to go along with this practice out of politeness.

Reference to future events, etc.

Any future event about which a Middle Easterner talks will invariably be prefaced by '*In Sha Allah*' – 'God willing'. This usage is still as common and widespread as the former use of 'D.V.' – 'Deo volente' – once was in the West, and it would be regarded as presumptuously impious not to use it. Likewise any reference to the birth or beauty of a child will be accompanied by the phrase '*Ma sha Allah*' – 'with God's grace'. On starting a journey many people will exclaim '*Bismillahi*' – 'In God's name'.

If someone sneezes in the Arab world, he will say '*Al hamdu lillah*' — 'Thanks be to God' — as thanks that evil has been averted.

Hospitality

The tradition of hospitality in the Arab world, perhaps deriving from the customs of the desert, is both ancient and enduring and this manifests itself in great generosity towards guests. The essential approach is summed up in a desert Bedu greeting:

> Oh guest of ours, though you have come,
> though you have visited us, and though
> you have honoured our dwellings, we
> verily are the real guests and you are
> the Lord of this house.

The Bedu attitude towards hospitality is more fully described in Appendix D.

Arab friends nowadays are always most generous in their hospitality in town as well as country following their old customs even in a twentieth century environment.

Tafaddal

The usual Arab custom among men is for each to say the equivalent of 'After you' – in Arabic '*Tafaddal*', i.e. 'be so good as (to go first)', when going into meals or through doors at functions in private houses. Guests should eventually yield on being given precedence, but it is polite first to offer to give way oneself. This custom does not extend to places of public resort like football stadiums!

However, men may wrestle mildly with one another sometimes in jest over who shall 'acquire the merit' of giving way to the other.

Appointments

People in the Arab world do not on the whole like to make appointments very much in advance and conversely they will often issue invitations to lunch or dinner very much at the last minute. A visitor, therefore, often cannot count on a cut-and-dried programme being made for him in advance, for this is not the normal Arab style.

Politeness on making calls, visiting, etc.

On greeting a person visited or a visitor there is often the customary handshake, an exchange of formal greetings, usually at some length, while standing and again after sitting down. One must always stand to greet anyone. The following subjects may be worked in at this stage:

usual openers like 'How do you do?' 'How are you?'
 (not 'Hallo' except to a very close friend)
pleasure at having opportunity of meeting
health
family and their health
enquiries about mutual friends
weather
journey
first impressions.

It is wise to let people speak without interruption, leaving one's points to be made later in reply.

Condolences

Sometimes it is appropriate to call on friends to offer condolences on the death of a close relation rather than to write, or in addition to a letter. In such cases one should establish where the senior relative of the deceased is sitting to receive people and go there. One may express condolence to the relatives one meets in one's own way or with some such phrases as 'May I present my condolences' or 'May God grant you consolation' (or one of the phrases suggested amongst Arabic phrases in Chapter 9. It is normal to sit in silence for a while and then to take one's leave. One may infer what to do on such occasions from the actions of others.

Chapter 8

Faux Pas

Superiority of Manner

The greatest faux pas in the Middle East are caused by a conscious, or unconscious, revelation that a Westerner considers his culture, manners and mores superior to, rather than merely differing from, those of the local people. A few examples, past and present will illustrate this point, most of them, as it happens, mentioned by warm friends of Britain and the West.

In 1952 a British master in a Cairo school with a majority of Egyptian children came into class and said 'Children I regret to have to inform you that the King is dead.' He meant King George VI and not King Farouk, then King of Egypt! Again in Cairo, Muslim children were kept in line outside the classroom at an English school while the Christian children attended prayers inside and, at yet another school in Egypt, it was compulsory for Egyptian boys to do Scottish sword dances (an exercise which incidentally did a future distinguished diplomat no harm!).

A recent book on the Arab World quoted an Englishman who was addressed as 'Sir' in Arabia, a normal and natural courtesy, as saying, 'In England, we don't call each other "Sir". That is very old fashioned.' This may be true in the main, but does rather presumptuously suggest that what goes in the U.K. ought also to go in the Middle East.

It is true that faux pas can be made in the opposite direction, as when the British Ambassador was summoned by a certain Egyptian Foreign Minister and instructed to remove V.R. from the devices shown on the British Embassy gates, because there was no longer a British Viceroy in Egypt.

Faux pas can arise through differing attitudes towards many matters. A remark by a foreigner may wound an Arab's sense of pride without the speaker being aware that he has caused any offence at all. This could arise, for example, from undue precision about a financial matter, which might be interpreted as showing lack of confidence or doubt in a man's integrity. What one side sees as efficiency may be seen as mistrust by the other.

Two true examples from many years ago show how words used and tone of voice can unwittingly cause misunderstanding and offence. A British officer was not satisfied with the manner in which an Arab officer was taking a parade. Eventually he threw his swagger stick on the ground in desperation, saying 'Oh, come on, Hassan Effendy!' Later in the day the British officer was astonished to be summoned before his Commanding Officer to explain why he had insulted the Arab. The young Arab officer had complained that, although he did not mind being called all the names in the military vocabulary, it was intolerable to be addressed: 'Come on!'

Another young Arab still struggling with his English was addressed in a gruff but kind manner: 'Come on Laddie, let us see if .....'. The youth took great offence because he had misheard the word 'Laddie' and thought he had been addressed as 'Lady'!

Differing attitudes towards time may cause difficulty, for hurrying is not a feature of the Middle East
and signs of impatience are not well regarded. Tap-
ping of the feet in impatience for example is regarded
as very bad manners and the maxim 'time is money'
would be regarded as very naïve and crude. Similarly
varying ideas about distance to be covered have also
been known to cause misunderstanding.

Patience

Patience is one of the virtues of the Middle East,
though it does not always show itself in street conduct
and in driving! In social and business matters it is
always shown , even though it may not be shown similarly to subordinates. It is not good form to show impatience in any social or business dealings, however
provoking.

Language

It is far from polite to assume, or even worse to mention, that it is incumbent on the people of the Middle
East to speak and do business in English without
accepting any concomitant obligation to use Arabic.
The fact that English is so widely spoken and used for
business and socially is a blessing, perhaps to be treated
with some humility.

Behaviour and Dress

It is equally arrogant and hence a faux pas to assume
that Western manners and modes of dress must auto-
matically be acceptable, or worse, ought to be accepted,
in the Middle East. There is a vast difference between
the mixed bathing beaches of Egypt and the Levant
and the austere customs in the Arabian Peninsula, but
in more places than not undue exposure, particularly
by girls and women, give offence, and the local view
of what may be worn may be very different from a
Westerner's. During the era of the miniskirt a young
British girl was wearing hers on a bus in Iran. An
elderly Iranian woman was so incensed that she seized
the girl's skirt and tried vigorously to pull it down to
reduce the area of leg so immodestly exposed. The old
lady was, however, so impetuous in her righteousness
that she nearly caused a more shocking revelation!

It may be asking too much to advise 'When in Rome,
do as the Romans do', but it is at least unwise to give
offence to the 'Romans'. In many areas of the Middle
East, particularly where it is customary for local
women to wear long robes concealing their bodies,
offence is given not only by the exposure of too much
flesh but also by women and girls wearing very tight
trousers and shorts. Should molestation result from
unsuitable clothing, or lack of it, the maxim "Volenti
non fit injuria" usually applies locally. Similarly, the
wearing of shorts by men is generally disliked and dis-
approved of in many parts of the Middle East.

Shoes

Other faux pas may be made in unexpected ways. A mosque may not be entered without removing one's shoes or putting on cloth overshoes, which are available at a small charge at many of the more famous mosques. It is, therefore, good form to take one's shoes off on entering a mosque before being asked to. Similarly, in Shaikhs' reception rooms (*majlises*), or private houses in the Arabian Peninsula, it is customary to remove one's shoes and it is a faux pas not to make any show of doing this, even if specifically invited later to keep them on.

Gestures and Actions

In some places parties, including lunches and dinners, are held sitting on the ground and it is regarded in the Middle East as a sign of pride and boorishness to point the soles of one's feet at any one. The fact that one may have done this without any comment being made does not mean that it has passed unnoticed. It is also very impolite not to rise if anyone, particularly someone senior, comes into a room or joins an assembly or meeting. Casual posture on some occasions may also attract unfavourable attention. It is a major faux pas, and almost certain to be misunderstood, if one beckons someone, underhand, in the manner usual in Britain, Europe and the U.S. Such a gesture has the same sort of connotations as the incorrect form of Churchill's famous wartime V sign. Much the same applies to the thumbs up sign. Beckoning in the Middle East has to be done by putting up the hand like a policeman halting traffic and then rolling all the fingers over together outward and overhand. Waving of the left hand in greeting is wrong. This, as with the handshake, must be done with the right hand.

Belching is never obligatory in the Arab world, but at a traditional Arab feast some guests will mark their appreciation by deep belches. Even if Sir Richard Burton, the eminent orientalist, wrote *A History of Farting*, nether explosions are quite taboo.

Names

It is, of course, bad form to use the term 'Christian name' to mean first or given name in an area predominantly Muslim. 'Is your Christian name Ahmad?' is a contradiction in terms; men with such names as Muhammad, Ahmad and Abdulla must be Muslim.

Admiration

It is a faux pas to express admiration of objects of beauty in a private house as the result may be that the host or person addressed my feel obliged to make a gift of the article in question. The European habit of expressing admiration as a compliment needs, therefore, to be kept in hand and judiciously modified, if embarrassment to both parties is to be avoided.

Food, Pork and Alcohol

Wherever food is eaten with the hand, it is, as has already been remarked, a faux pas to use the left hand, which is used for unclean purposes and under no circumstances must be plunged into a communal bowl or dish, though it may be used in peeling fruit. It is, of course, a major faux pas to offer any Muslim pork, ham or bacon as this is expressly prohibited by the Koran and a Muslim should never be pressed to take an alcoholic drink, as many but not all Muslims interpret the Koran as forbidding this.

Undue Familiarity

Assumption that, in address and general behaviour, the egalitarian style of the Anglo-Saxons is acceptable in the Middle East may also be a faux pas and it is as well to use courtesy titles, whether Shaikh, Sayyid, Mister, Mrs, Monsieur or Madame until close relations are established.

Pronunciation

There are certain mispronunciations which are faux pas: for instance, to pronounce Shaikh (Sheikh) as if it were 'Chic'; the correct pronunciation is like 'Shake' with the terminal sound as in the Scottish 'loch' instead of the 'k' sound; to pronounce 'Harim' as if it were

'Hairem' instead of 'Hareem'; and to pronounce 'Fakir' as if it were 'Faker' instead of 'Fakeer'.

Misconceptions

Misconceptions about the term 'Harim' are, if displayed, faux pas. The Harim is not, as film fantasies might lead one to suppose, the place where rich Shaikhs keep their fancy women. On the contrary, the word denotes something sacrosanct and meriting respect, a respect always given by the Bedu tribes to the women and children of their enemies and captives. The word 'Harim' generally means, therefore, the Muslim's wife and female members of his family, who, as such, must in all circumstances be respected. It also is applied to their living quarters.

Aberrations

Certain forms of behaviour are clearly faux pas, for instance if a Scotsman decides to wear a kilt with the traditional lack of underwear at a party where he may have to squat on the ground. Equally, it is wrong to assume that European shorts and short sleeves will be as acceptable in a respectable Arab household or an official's residence as they might be on the beach.

If one fails to shake the small coffee cup offered by a servant in the Arabian Peninsula when one has had enough – two or three cups are considered polite – the servant following the laws of hospitality is bound to go on refilling it. Classically, failure to shake the cup at the appropriate moment is therefore a faux pas, but servants nowadays are often understanding and may not press coffee on one. It is equally wrong, however, to emulate the lady traveller who, told that she must shake the coffee cup to stop the hospitable flow, thought that shaking was the invariable method of indicating satiety. Consequently when her host pressed her to eat more, which all good Arab hosts do, with some such words as, 'But you have eaten nothing', she shook the whole round tray on which the rice and meat had been set out, albeit with some difficulty!

Chapter 9

Arabic Phrases

Greetings

As salam alaikum	Peace be on you
Sabah al Khair	Good morning
Kaif halak? (Izaiak in Egypt)	How are you?
Misa al Khair	Good evening
Marhaba	Greetings

Farewells

Ma salaama	Goodbye
Fi aman Illah	Goodbye

Congratulations

Mabruk	Congratulations
Al Id mubarak	Congratulations on the Id festival

Please, Sorry, etc.

Min fadlak	Please
Arjuk	Please (I pray you)
Al afu (afwan)	I beg your pardon. Sorry.
Ma alaish	I am sorry (also it does not matter)
Ma yukhalif	It does not matter

Thanks

Shukran	Thanks
Ashkurak	Thank you
Mashkur	Thank you
Sufra daima	Thanks for a meal (may your table always be spread)

Condolences

Allah yarhamu	May God grant pardon
Ad dawam lillah	Eternity is God's
Ahsan Allah Azakum	May God grant you solace

General

Zain	Good (general)
Kuwais	Good (Egyptian)

In sha Allah   I hope so (God willing)

Al hamdu lillah   Praise be to God (used
e.g. as 'very well thanks'
to an enquiry 'How are
you?')

Bass   Enough

Tafaddal   Be so good as to (e.g. take
precedence or go ahead)

Appendix A

I. Muslim Schools of Jurisprudence

HANIFI

Abu Hanifa, whose real name was Al-Naaman ibn Thabit and who worked in Iraq dying in 767 A.D./150 AH, set down a system of rules to embody the answer to all possible questions of Islamic law and the Hanifite system now has the majority of Sunnis as adherents.

HANBALI

Ahmad ibn Hanbal, who was born in Baghdad and died in 855 AD/241 AH, wrote a major work called *Musnad*, a collection of 30,000 traditions. In brief this is the strictest school, attaching primary weight to the Koran as a source of positive law and less to the Hadith. Adherents of his teaching now come mainly from Najd in Saudi Arabia, Qatar and the Sunnis in Oman and the United Arab Emirates as well as North Western parts of the Indian subcontinent.

MALIKI

Malik ibn Anas who died in 795 AD/179 AH, was a citizen of Madina, though he had influence with Haroun al Rashid the Abbasid Caliph (786-809 AD). His teachings found official recognition throughout northern Africa and was introduced to Spain under the

Umayyads. It prevails nowadays in Upper Egypt, the Sudan, the whole of North Africa, the United Arab Emirates, Bahrain and Kuwait.

SHAFI

Muhammad ibn Idris al Shafi spent his childhood in Makkah and could reputely recite the Koran at the age of seven. He had influence at the court of the Caliphs in Baghdad but moved to Egypt, where he died. He maintained the infallibility of an unanimous agreement within the Muslim community at any given time. The Shafis are now found in Lower Egypt, parts of the Levant, East and Southern Africa, Western and Southern Arabia, India and Indonesia and Malaysia.

WAHHABI (MUWAHHIDI – UNITARIAN)

In Saudi Arabia the majority of the people are followers of the school of Muhammad ibn Abd al Wahhab, a great reformer of the mid 18th century who followed the school of Ahmad ibn Hanbal. Commonly known as Wahhabis, they prefer the term Muwahhidun – Unitarians – and they are very strict and purist in their beliefs and practices.

IBADHI

In Oman and parts of North Africa, the majority follow the Ibadhi *madhab* based on the doctrines of Abdulla ibn Ibadh who first came to prominence in Iraq around 683 AD/64 AH. The Ibhadis claim, therefore, that their *madhab* came into being over a century before the orthodox schools.

ZAIDI

The Zaidi sect was founded by Zaid ibn Ali ibn Hussain, who lived in the eighth century and was a great grandson of Ali, the Prophet Muhammad's son-in-law. The Zaidis, who are found mainly in Yemen, follow a doctrine advocating a simple puritan mode of life.

GENERAL

The generally accepted rule in Arab countries is that every Muslim is governed by the particular *madhab* to which he belongs.

II. Some Islamic Terms

Jama	Mosque
Masjid	Mosque
Kibla (Qibla)	The direction of Makkah
Mihrab	Niche in a mosque pointing in the direction of Makkah, where the Imam leads the prayers
Minaret	The tower of the mosque
Minba	Pulpit in a mosque
Imam	The leader of prayers in the mosque
Muezzin	The man who calls the people to prayer from the Minaret
Kadi (Qadi, Qadhi)	Muslim Judge of the Sharia law
Mufti	Muslim legislator

Appendix B

Names of Ruling Families in the Arab World

Al Saud	Saudi Arabia
Hashemite	Jordan
Al bu Said	Oman
Al Sabah	Kuwait
Al Khalifa	Bahrain
Al Thani	Qatar
Al Nahayyan	Abu Dhabi
Al Maktum	Dubai
al Qasimi (Qawasim)	Sharjah and Ras al Khaimah
al Naimi	Ajman
al Mualla	Umm al Qawain
al Sharqi	Fujairah

Al, with a capital A, denotes 'the people or family of' and is to be distinguished from al, with a small a, meaning 'the'. Thus Al bu Said, Al Sabah, etc. denotes the name of the founder of the ruling family (Said, Sabah, etc.) The al with a small a is adjectival and descriptive.

Appendix C

Addresses of Royal Protocol Officers

JORDAN   H.E. The Head of Royal Protocol
The Royal Palace
Amman

MOROCCO   H.E. The Minister of the
     Morocco Court
The Royal Palace
Rabat

OMAN   H.E. The President of the
     Diwan of H.M. for Protocol
The Palace
Muscat

SAUDI ARABIA   H.E. the Chief of Royal Protocol
The Royal Palace
Riyadh

Honorifics

Jalala   Majesty
Simu al Malaki   Royal Highness
Simu   Highness

Siada (President and Ministers in some countries)	Excellency
Maali (generally Ministers)	
Saada (generally Ambassadors and sometimes senior officials)	
Fakhama	Excellency

Appendix D

Bedu Hospitality

This is well described by Colonel H.R.P. Dickson in his book *The Arab of the Desert*:

A guest is, of course, expected not to impose on his host nor take advantage of the laws of hospitality unless he genuinely requires food and rest. A traveller, for instance, at the end of a long day's journey, will look round for a tent where he can spend the night and finding one in the distance, can legitimately go to it and get a night's food and lodging. Should he, however, be within a mile or two of his own destination, he must make an effort and complete the distance rather than sponge on perhaps poor strangers.

In the desert a man (or party) does not brazenly go up to a tent and demand hospitality. That is never done. Gentlemanly instincts are highly developed in the Badawin. A man approaches the tents of a prospective host honestly and with becoming diffidence. He must draw near from the front end and not from the back of a tent or tents of his hosts – in other words he must come up on the side where the tents are open and facing him. He must then make his camel kneel a couple of hundred yards away, and then must busy himself with its saddlery or start tying his camel's knees up ... until he is noticed. The host will then either go out himself from his tent, and invite the traveller to come and rest, or he will send out a servant, according as he thinks the man is a more or less important person.

The guest will then be conducted to the guest's part of the tent, will be given coffee, a meal and a night's rest, and will depart in the early morning. This normal form of entertaining a guest in the desert is exercised every day. It may be called giving a traveller a 'night's rest' but the guest never dreams of offering payment nor would such offer be accepted.

Appendix E

Traditional Arab Entertaining

It is rare, nowadays, to be entertained to a meal where food is presented on the ground, but this is still fairly frequent in areas not yet affected by more sophisticated ideas. There is a particular pleasure and intimacy in eating in this style and, if one is lucky enough to be invited to a small meal of this sort, one may sit on the ground with food set out on a cloth in bowls and sample beautifully cooked rice, a roast, or sometimes boiled, sheep or goat, dishes of broth, chicken, chops and vegetables in sauce followed by fresh fruit, dates and in some countries halwa, a distinctive sweetmeat. On such occasions only the right hand may be dipped into the communal bowls, the left hand in Arabia being used for unclean purposes.

If the classical Arab tradition is followed at a small or a great occasion, coffee, perhaps preceded by a cold, soft drink, will be served and likewise it will often be served after the meal, though in some cases the gathering breaks up as soon as the meal is over. If the full procedure of hospitality is followed, e.g. in the Arabian Peninsula, coffee, rosewater and incense will be served, after which leave should be taken immediately, for the Arab proverb runs 'After the incense there is to be no lingering on!'

If food is to be eaten with the hands, a bowl together with soap and towel will be brought for washing both before and after the meal, but in modern houses there is often a special wash place which one is invited to use.

The Arab tradition is to take off one's shoes or sandals when entering the house. This custom is less rigid nowadays, particularly when the entertaining is of a sophisticated nature or involves people other than Arabs; and it does not apply at all in the great cities of the Middle East. However, if the gathering is a small one – in the Arabian Peninsula – it is wise to watch what one's host or other guests do.

Misapprehensions

Certain misapprehensions about food in Arabia can be eliminated from the mind. Many years ago a senior British official is said to have been invited to a banquet by an important Shaikh. His wife, Lady ..... accompanied him as European women were sometimes treated as 'honorary men'! The Shaikh during the meal plucked the eye of the sheep, the whole carcass of which was set before him on a huge round dish, and handed it to the British official with some such words as 'We in Arabia are a people with our old customs and the most honoured guest must be offered the eye!' The British grandee took it and said 'Oh, Shaikh, I thank you sincerely and deeply. We in England are also people with our old customs and in our country the rule is "Ladies First", saying which he passed the sheep's eye to his wife! History does not relate what then happened, for the story is apocryphal.

The author knows of no case of a sheep's eye being specifically offered and enquiry in the Gulf area has produced the retort that it is not the custom and might only be done to tease a European. Among one or two tribes, however, the eye may be eaten together with the brains and other parts of the head. The old custom among some Arab people (e.g. Oman), however, is that the sheep's head is placed on the dish in front of the guest of honour, who is invited to crack the skull to release the brain for the company to eat.

The myth about the sheep's eye is, nonetheless, a hoary and popular one and according to an account in his biography by Stanton Hope, a Briton who became a Muslim, Hajji Williamson, played a practical joke on a visiting officer. He accompanied a party of British officials, led by a Captain Smith, to visit a Gulf Ruler. Captain Smith confided his dislike of the idea of having to eat the sheep's eye at dinner. Hajji Williamson who, by then, had been living with Arabs for 35 years, told him that there was no need to do so and instructed the young captain fully in tribal etiquette. Captain Smith remained unconvinced and Hajji Williamson, feeling a trifle piqued, deliberately informed the Shaikh that his chief guest regarded the eyes as the most succulent part of the sheep. The Shaikh was astonished. But, following Hajji's prompting, offered sheep's eyes to Captain Smith several times during the meal. Later a plateful of eyes was sent to the Captain's tent!

Appendix F

Muslim Marriage

A Muslim wedding takes a different form from a Christian one, where the wedding service, the most significant and binding event, is attended by the guests.

Islam allows a man to have four wives at one time, but the Koran imposes the difficult duty of treating them 'equally', not merely fairly. A Muslim man may marry a Christian or Jewish girl instead of a Muslim: the criteria is that she should be a *Kitabiya*, that is a woman professing one of the monotheistic religions based on their respective scriptures. A man may divorce a woman by saying three times to her 'I divorce you', but the matter does not rest there for the Muslim (*Sharia*) Courts have jurisdiction in all personal cases and will adjudicate on such matters as custody of children, alimony and disposal of the dowry. The three words repeated three times may prove very costly for a man.

A traditional Muslim marriage is negotiated between the parents of bride and bridegroom, usually through an intermediary and the negotiation covers dowry, bride price and other material matters. When all is agreed and bride and groom have consented, a date is fixed for the marriage contract (*agd az zawaj* or *agd an nika*) and the ceremonies.

Marriage customs vary from country to country but the marriage contract is usually the formal offer and acceptance, in the presence of two witnesses, of the terms previously agreed between the parties. Very often this contract is signed and sealed before a Kadi. Traditionally the bride does not appear in person. This ceremony is the legally binding part of the whole proceedings. Guests are seldom invited to witness this but, if a foreign guest were invited, he would be told precisely what to do.

The wedding celebrations last three days and three nights and there are festivities in the homes of both the bride and the groom. In the case of very important and rich personalities there may be public celebrations too, at which in many areas there will be strict segregation of the sexes. Westerners who are friends of the families concerned are often invited to these celebrations. Sometimes too westerners may be invited nowadays to wedding parties held in a European capital.

Appendix G

Some Arab Foods

MEAT (LAHM)

Dijaj (jidad)	Chicken
Hamam	Pigeon
Hubara	Bustard
Kuzi (Quzi)	Stuffed lamb
Wizz	Duck

FISH (SAMAK)

RICE

Aish	Rice (Saudi Arabia and Gulf)
Ruzz	Rice (much of Arabia)

BREAD

Khubz	Bread
Aish	Bread (generally 'aish' meaning what one lives on)
Aish baladi	Unleavened bread

MADE UP DISHES

Boraik	Meat in very light pastry
Burghul	Cracked wheat
Hiraiz	A wheat dish with egg
Hummus	Chick peas made into a sauce with sesame
Kafta	Meat balls
Mashwi	Something stuffed and baked, e.g. tomatoes, egg plant, courgettes
Tabouli	A salad with cracked wheat, parsley, onions, tomatoes, olive oil, lemon, etc.
Tahina	A thick sauce of sesame

PUDDINGS AND SWEETS

Baclawa	A rich sweet pastry
Muhallabia	Rice pudding
Umm Ali	Rice pudding with currants, etc.

This is very much a random list, but may help a little by mentioning some of the foods frequently met with.